Hi, My name is Royyan, and i am taking you on an adventure. Are you ready?

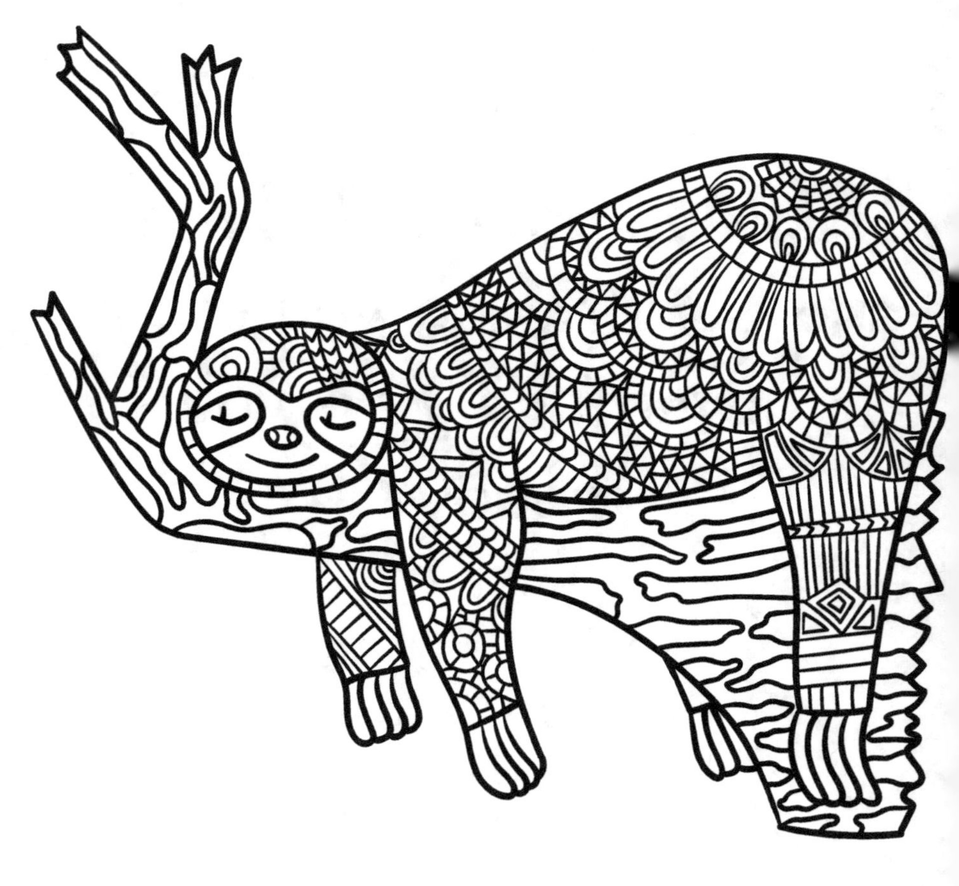

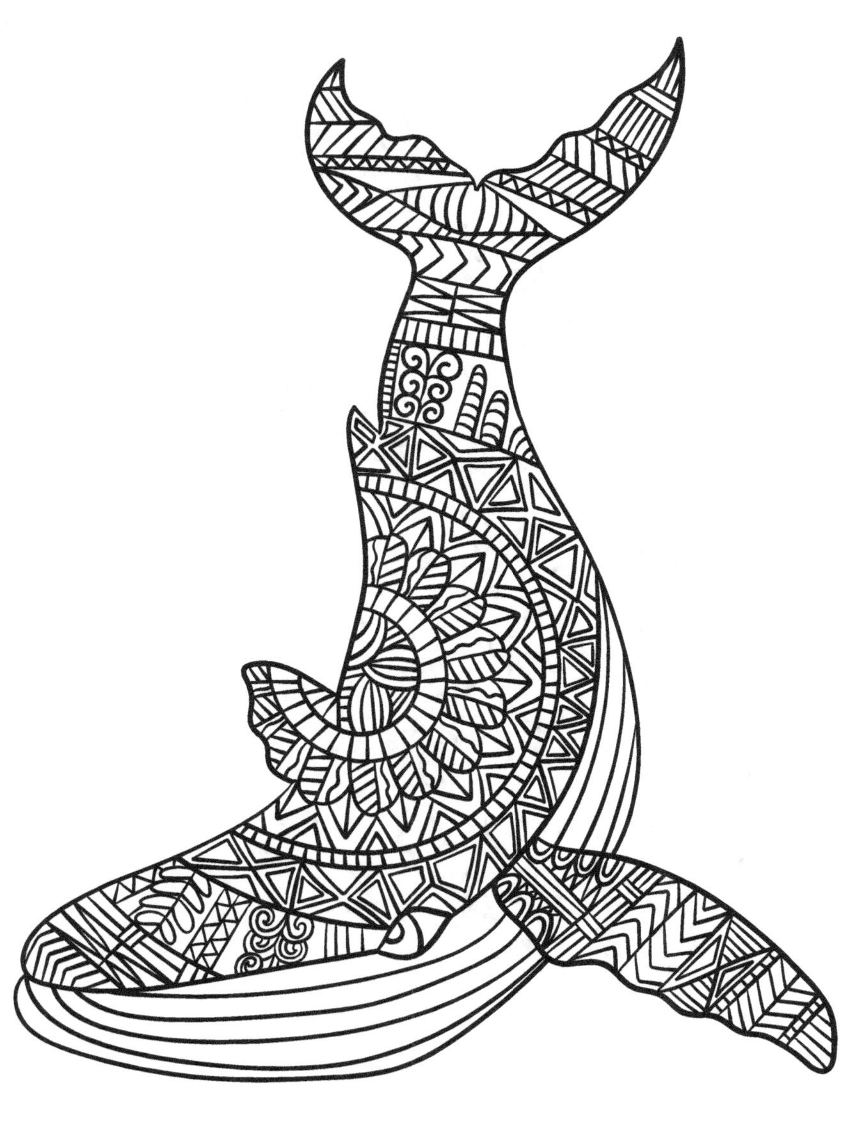

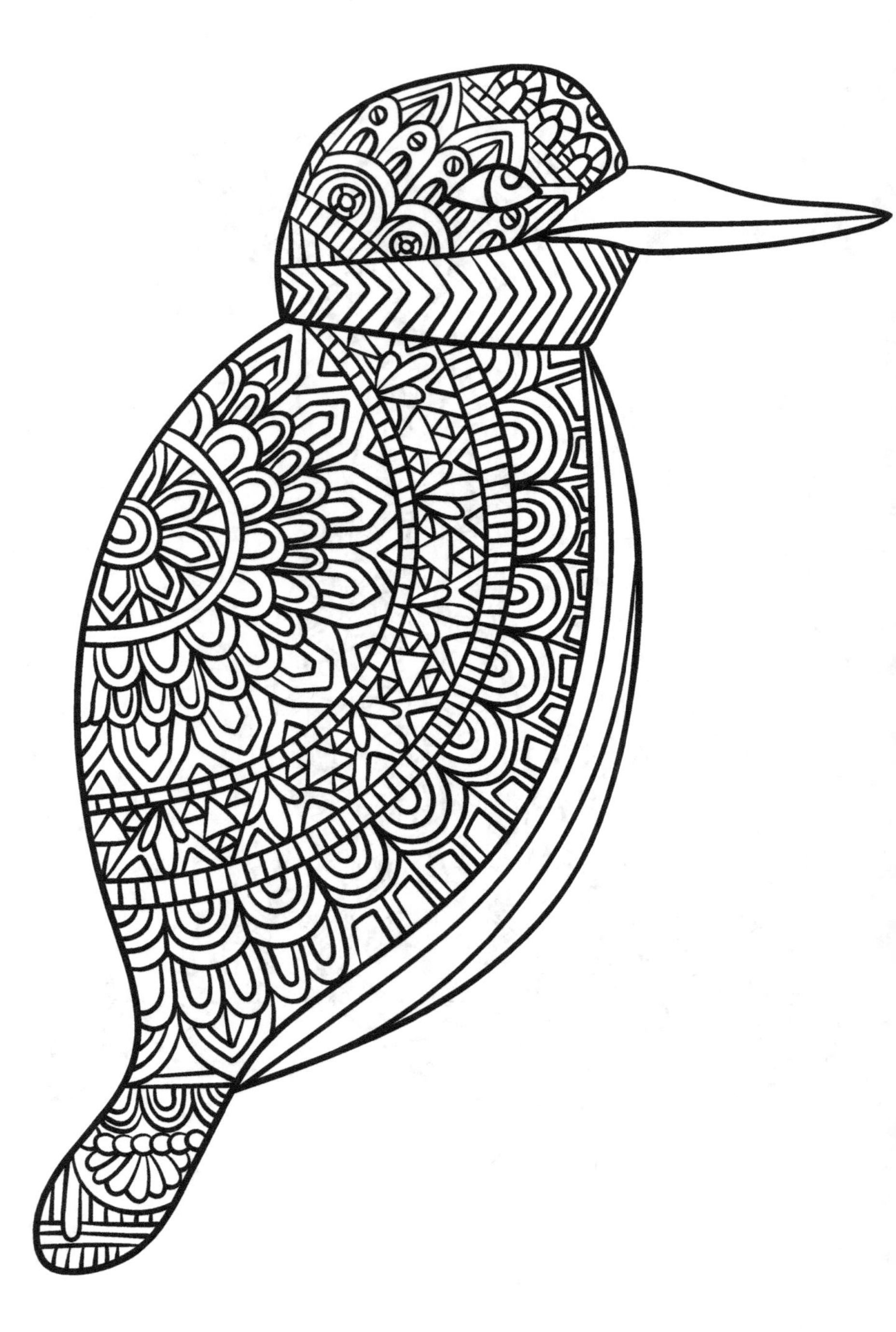

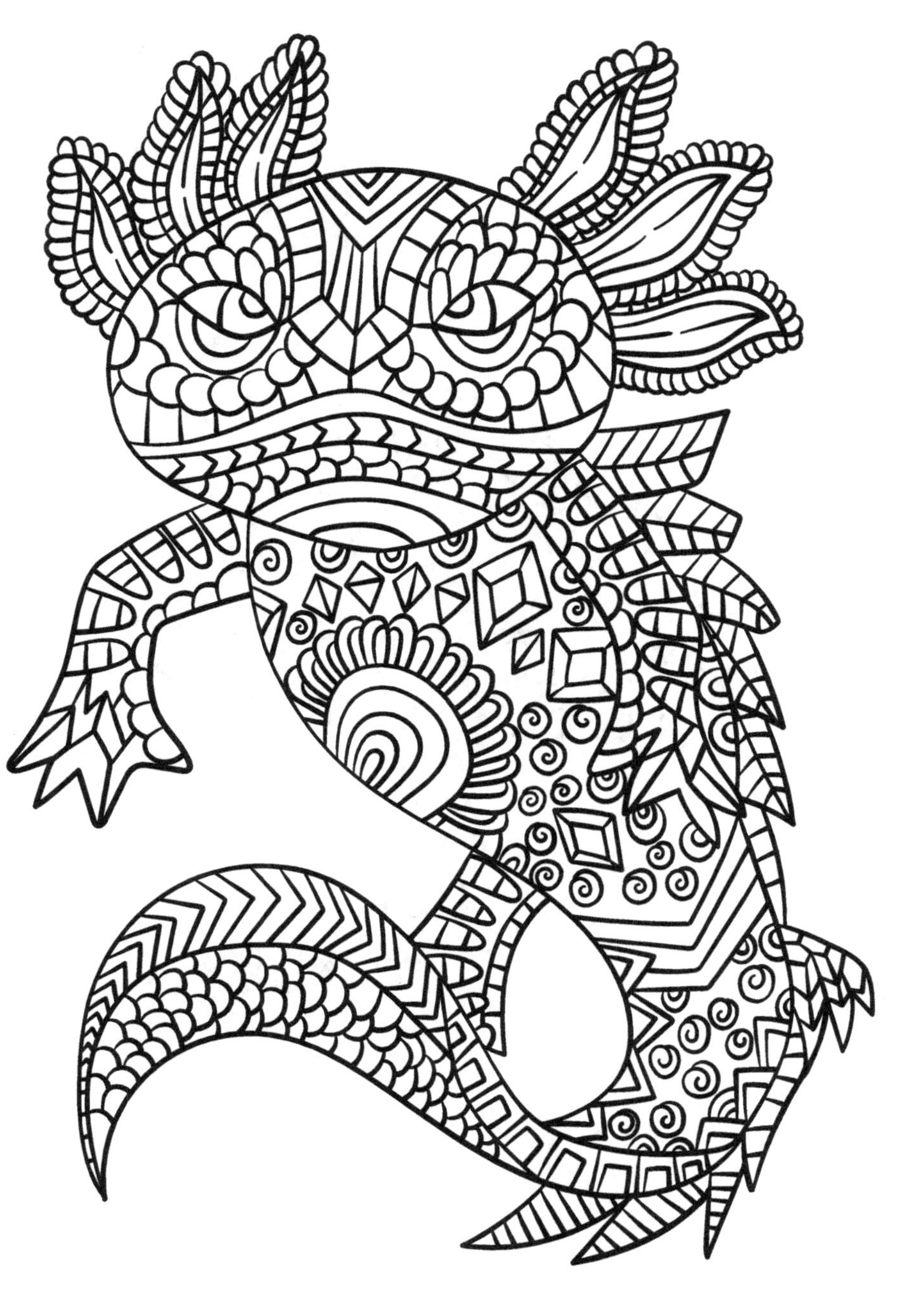

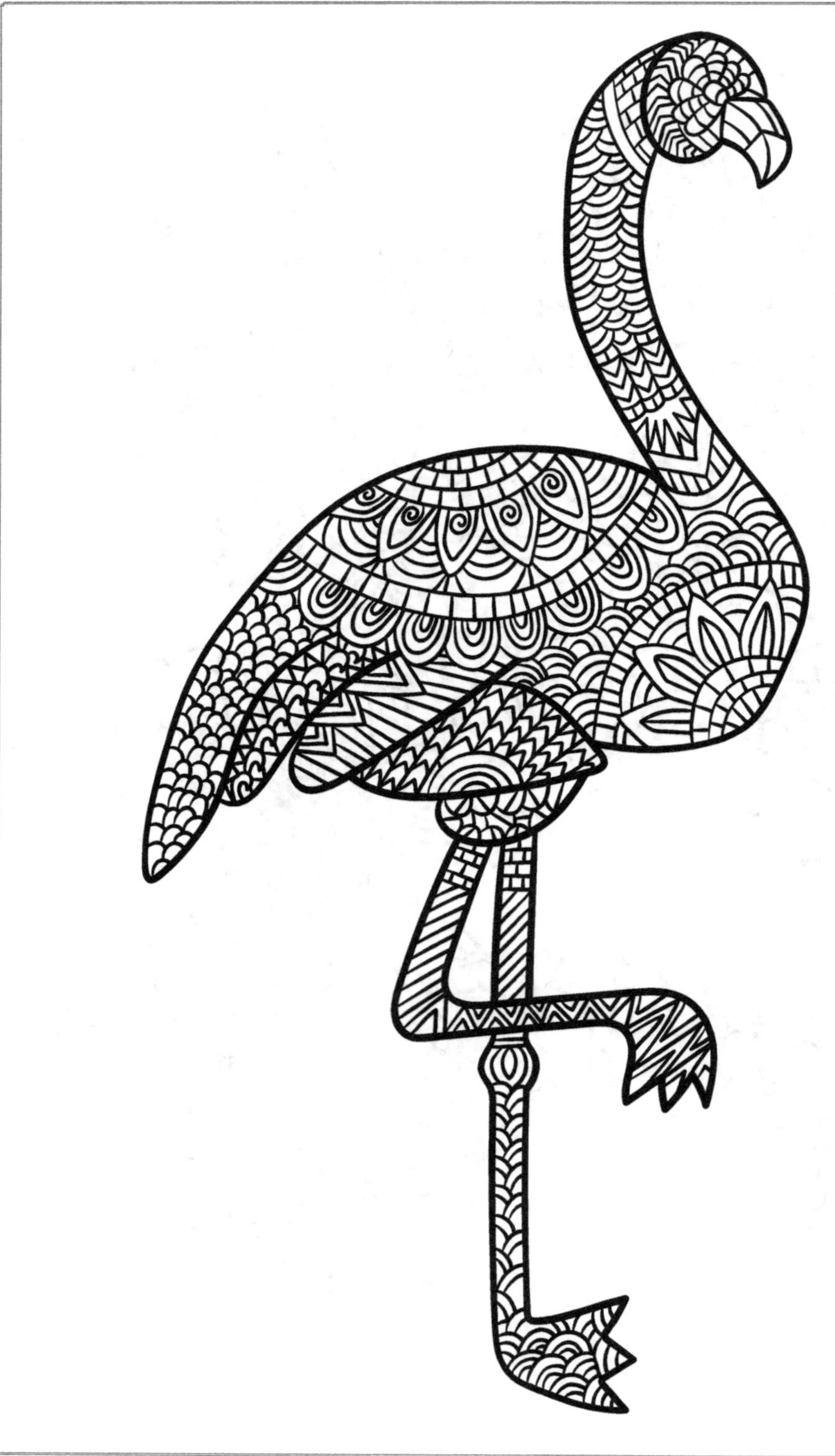

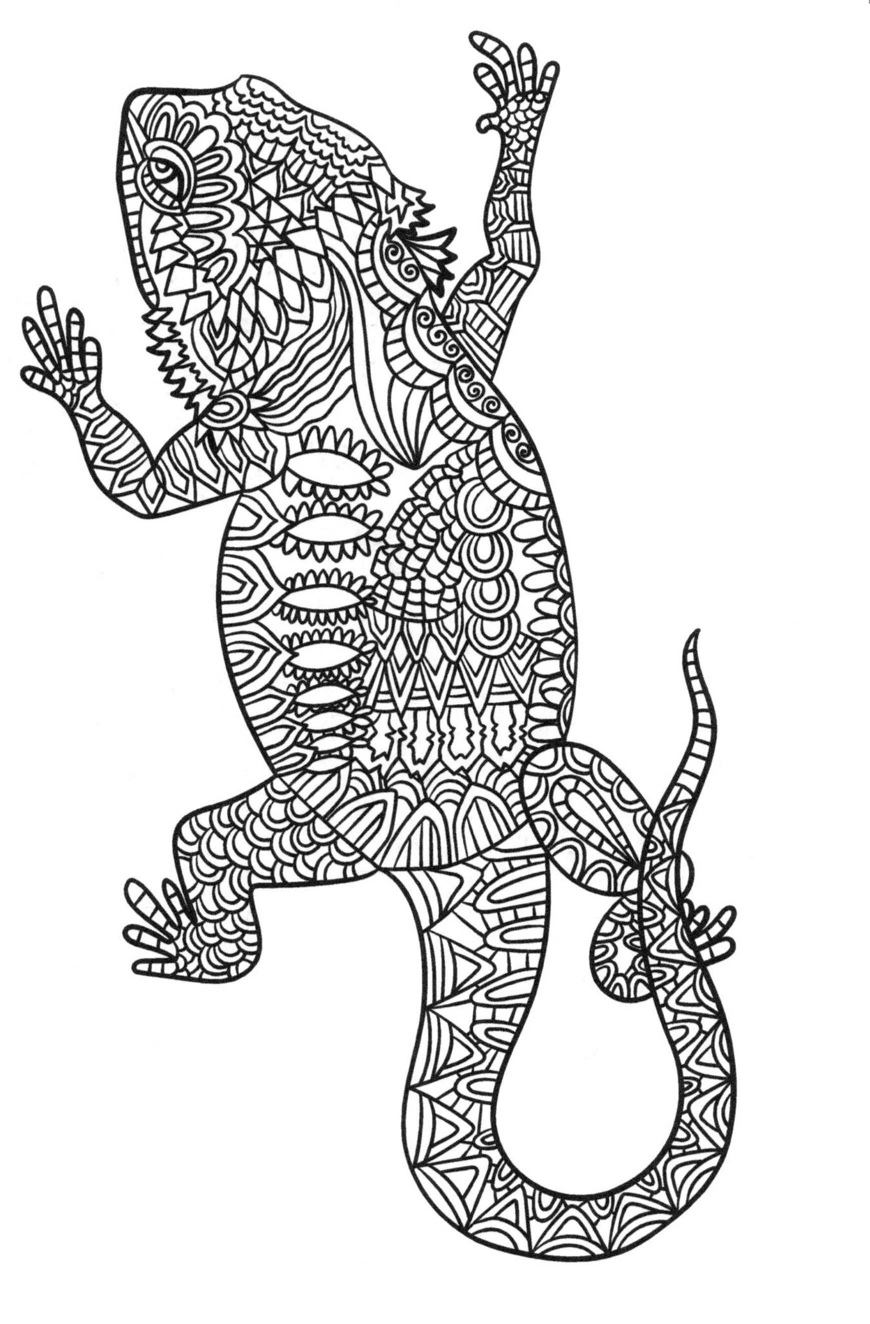

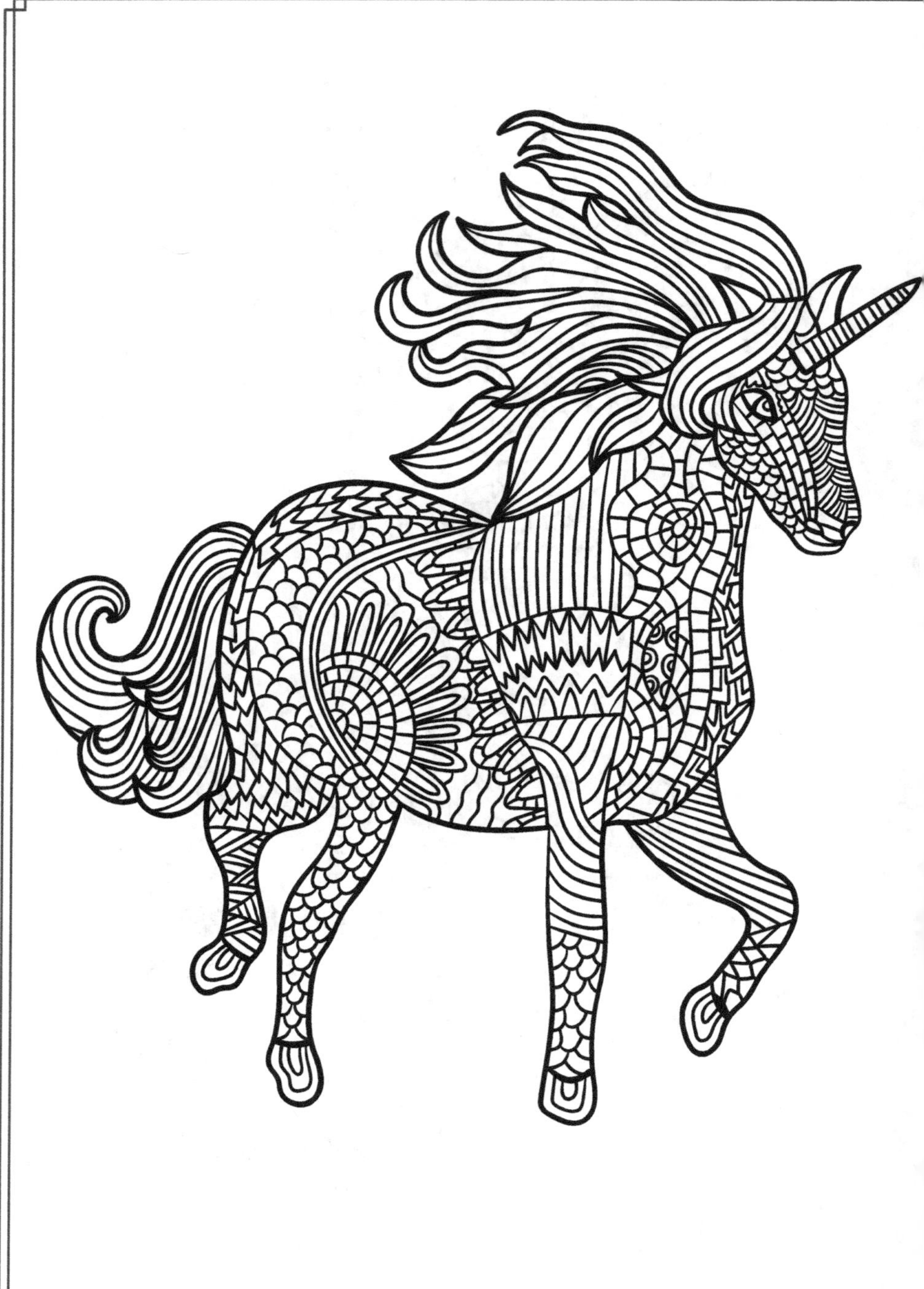

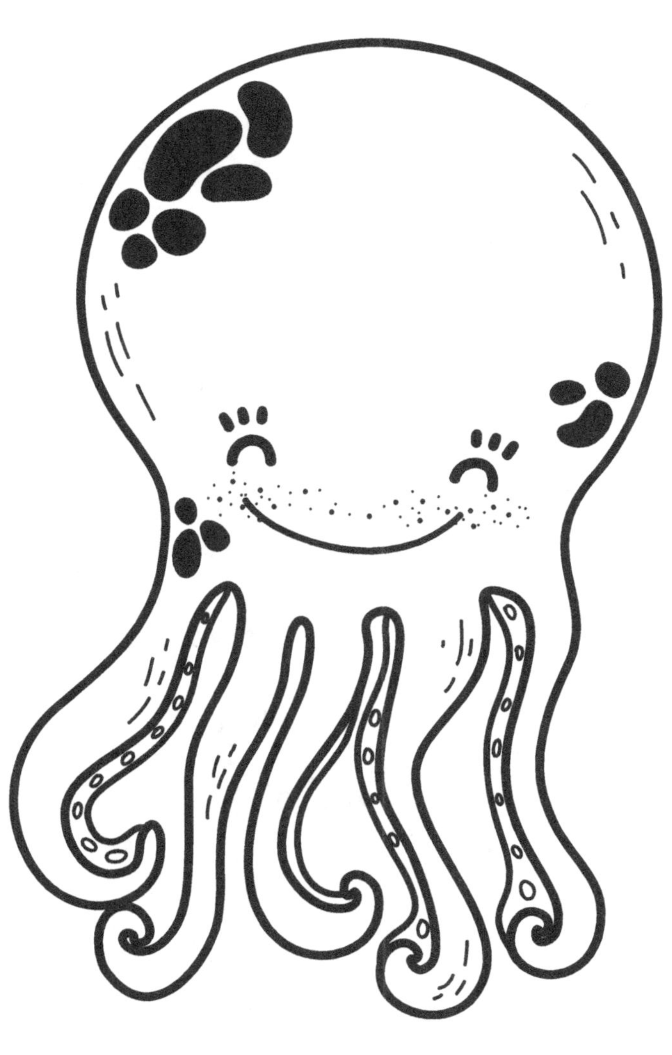

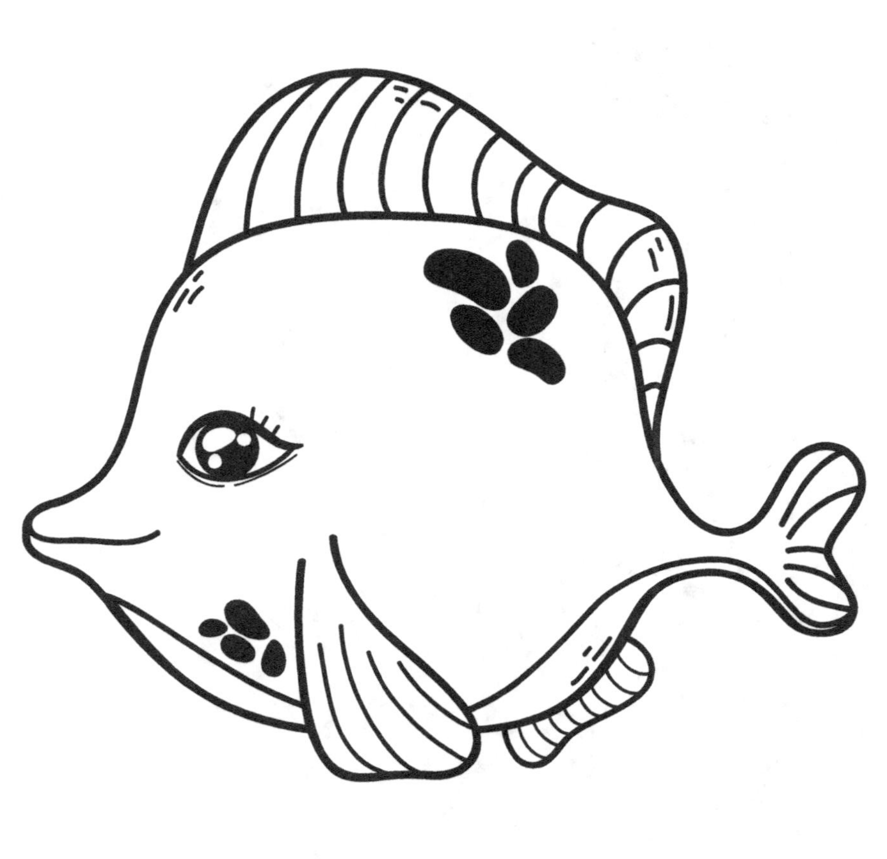

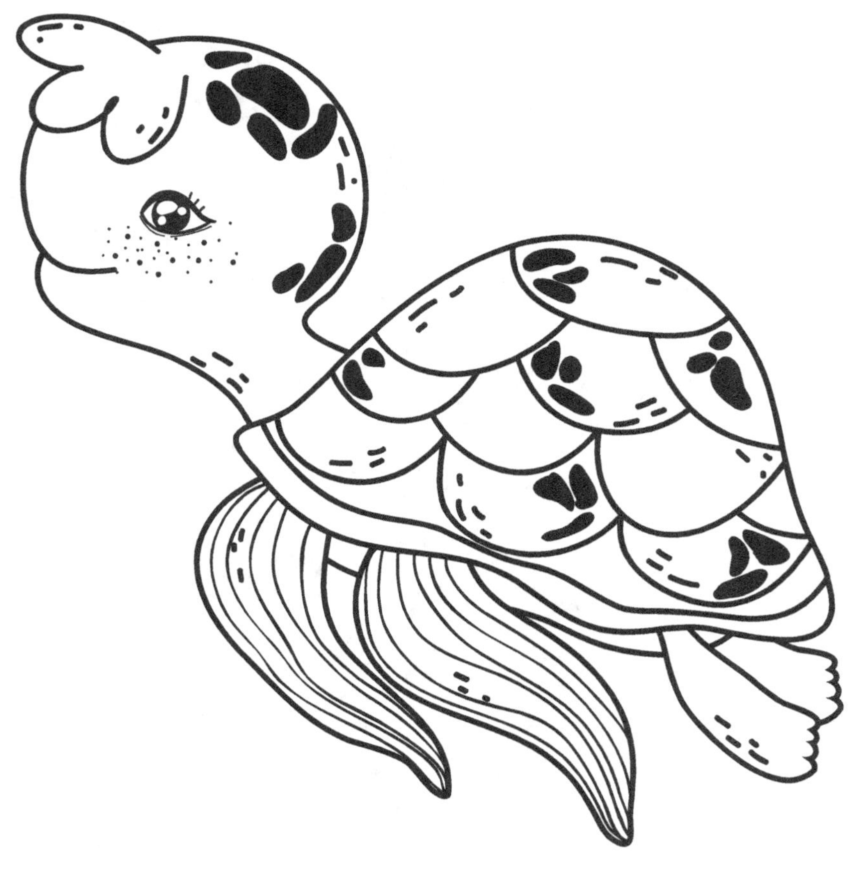

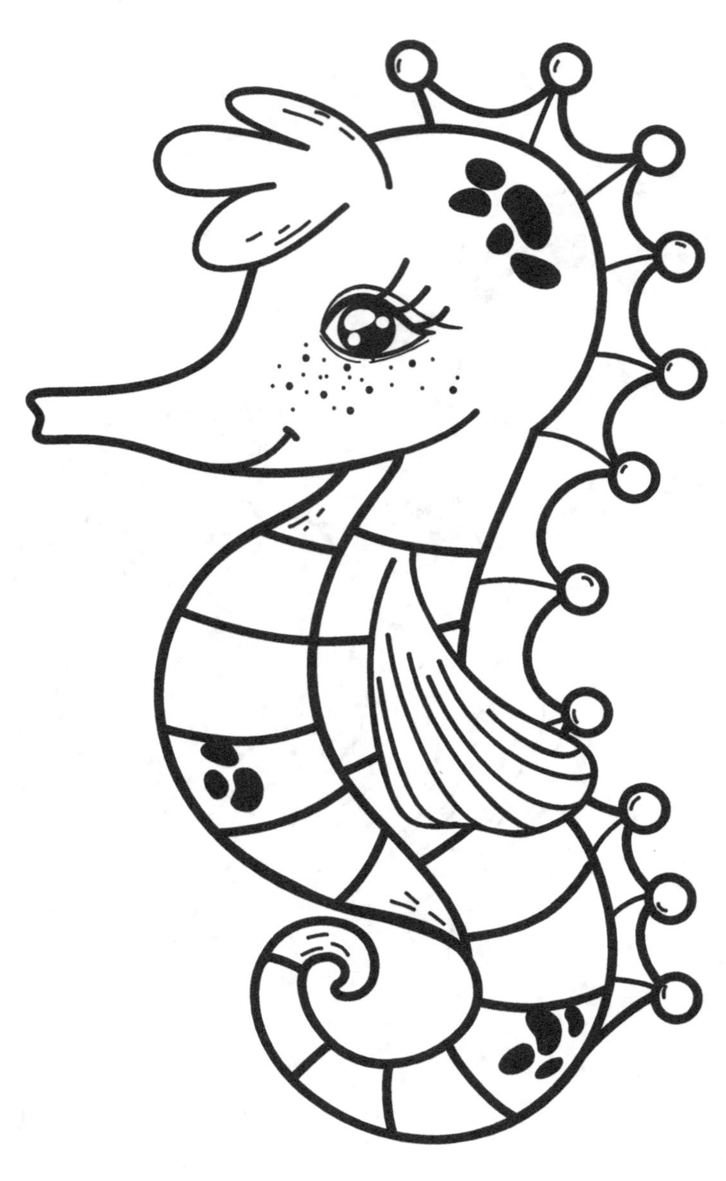

Now that we have gone this far, Let's identify some dinosaurs and paint them. Are you ready?

giganotosaurus

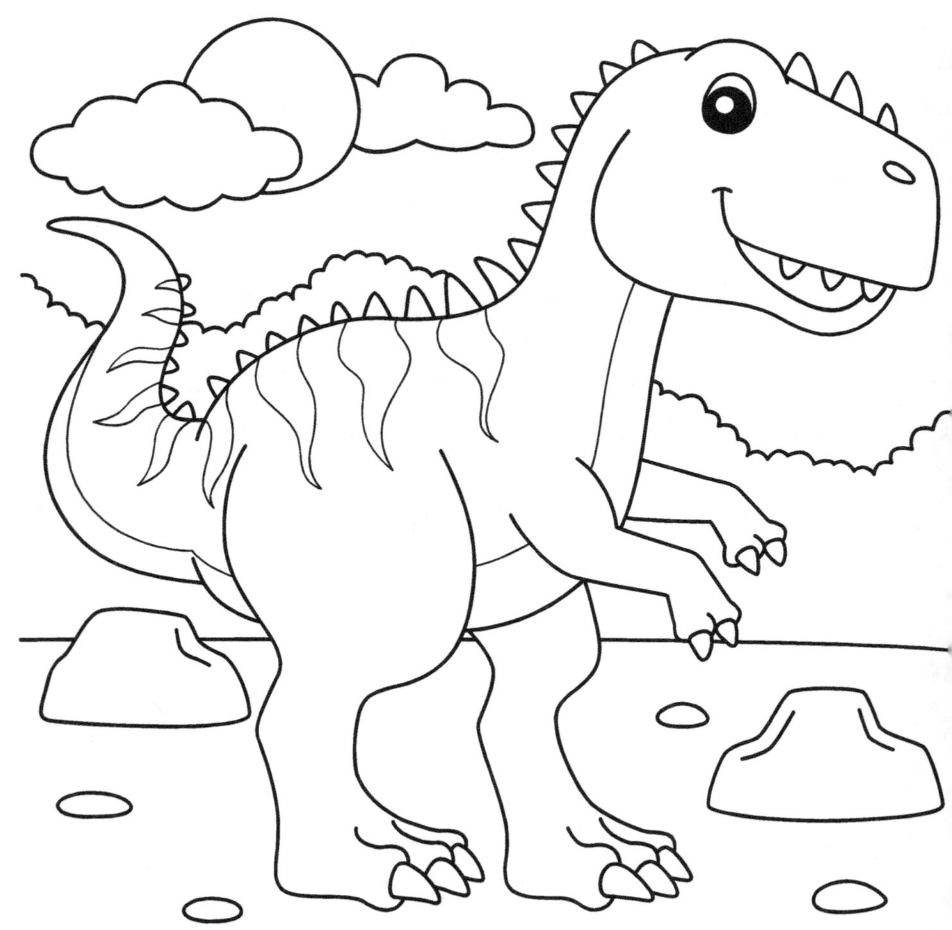

A giganotosaurus's head
was 6 feet long!

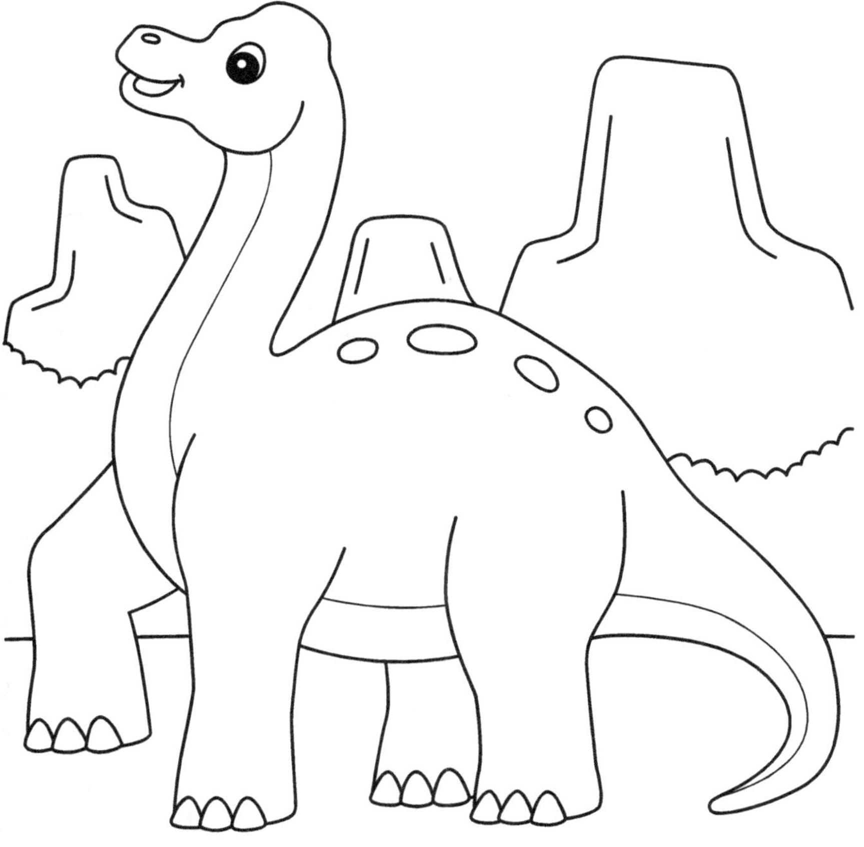

A brachiosaurus
lived 150 million
years ago.

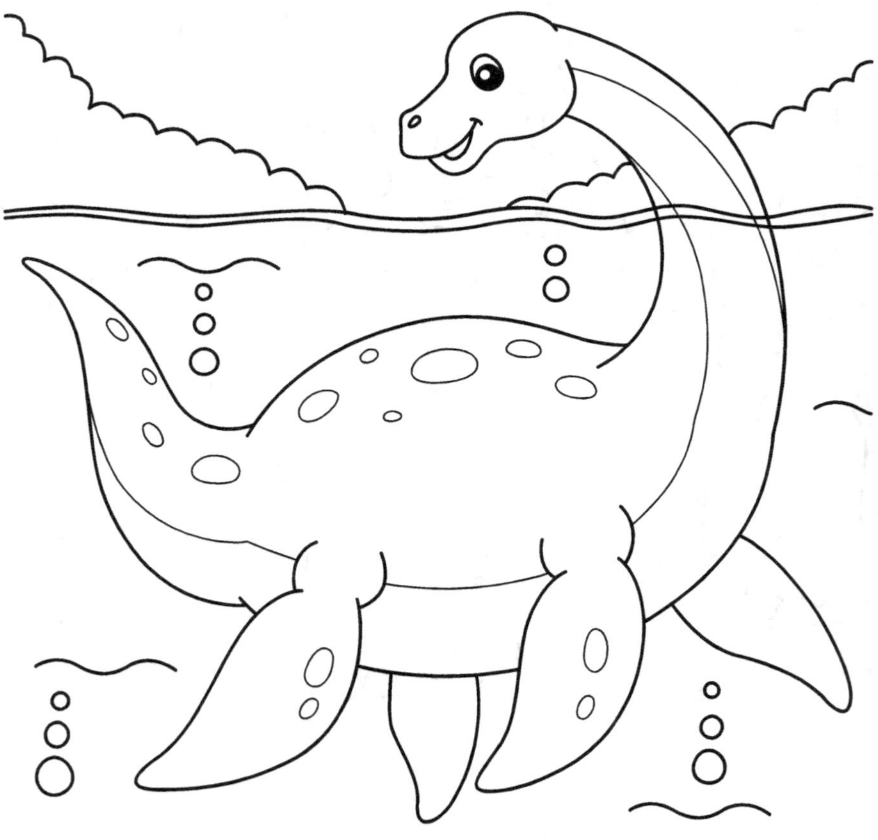

A plesiosaurus was a marine reptile.

xenoeratops

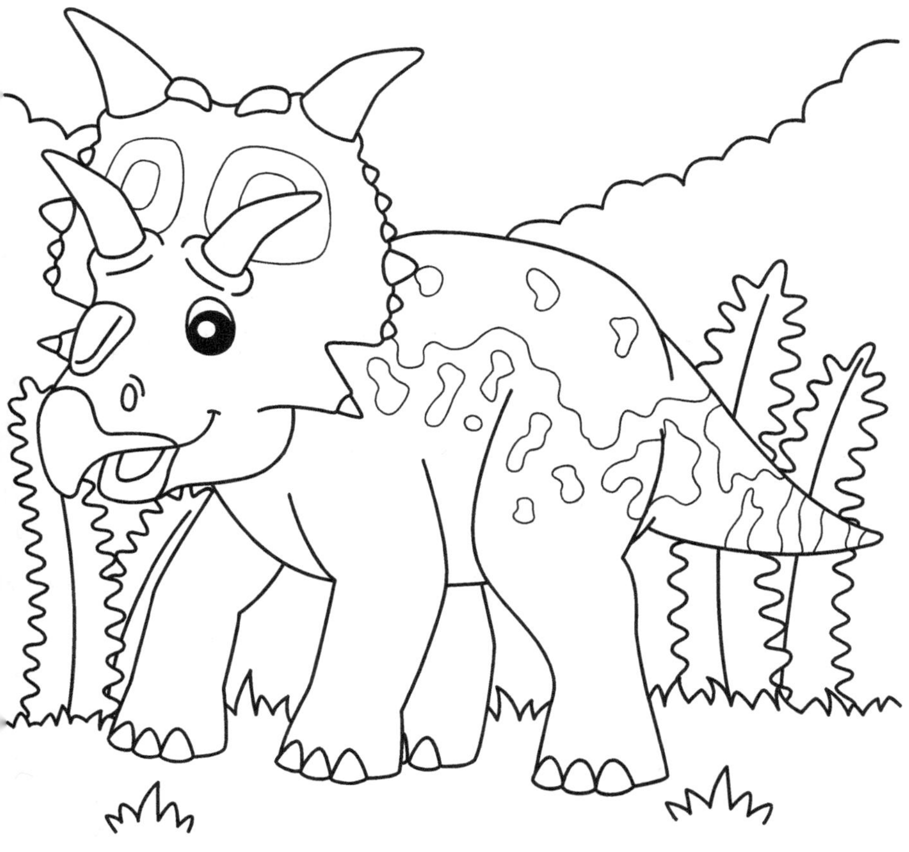

A xenoeratops's mouth was
shaped like a turtle.

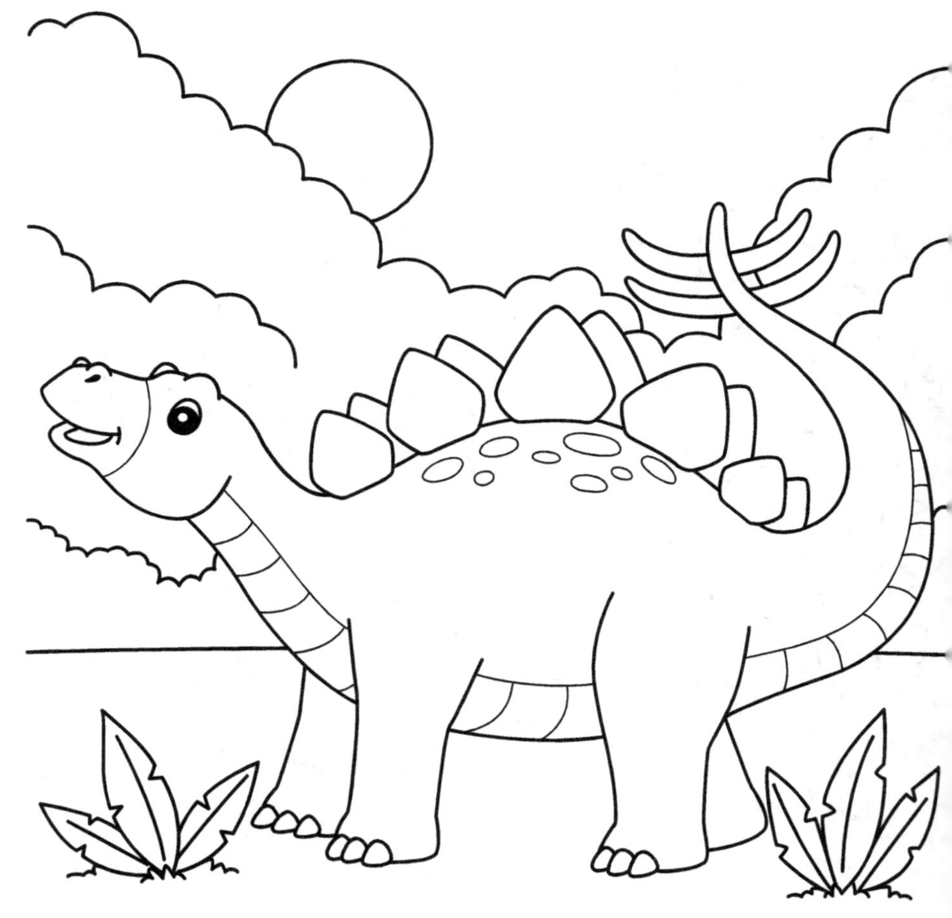

A stegosaurus's brain was
the size of a walnut.

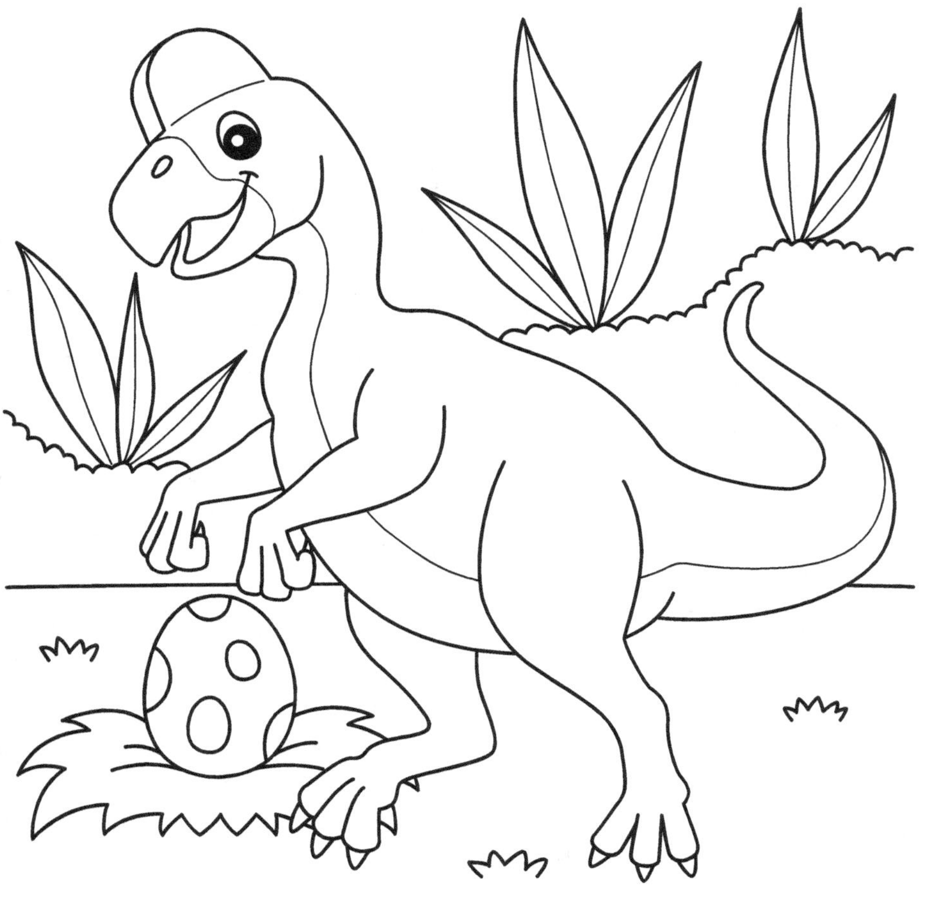

An oviraptor could lay up to
20 eggs at a time.

yangchuanosaurus

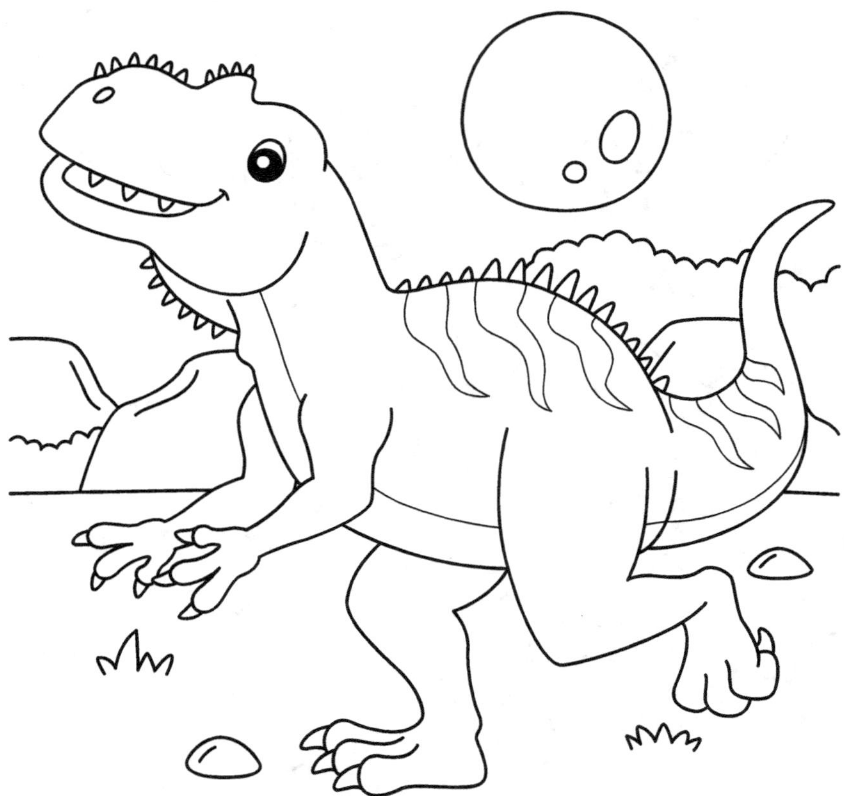

A yangchuanosaurus was as long as three car lengths.

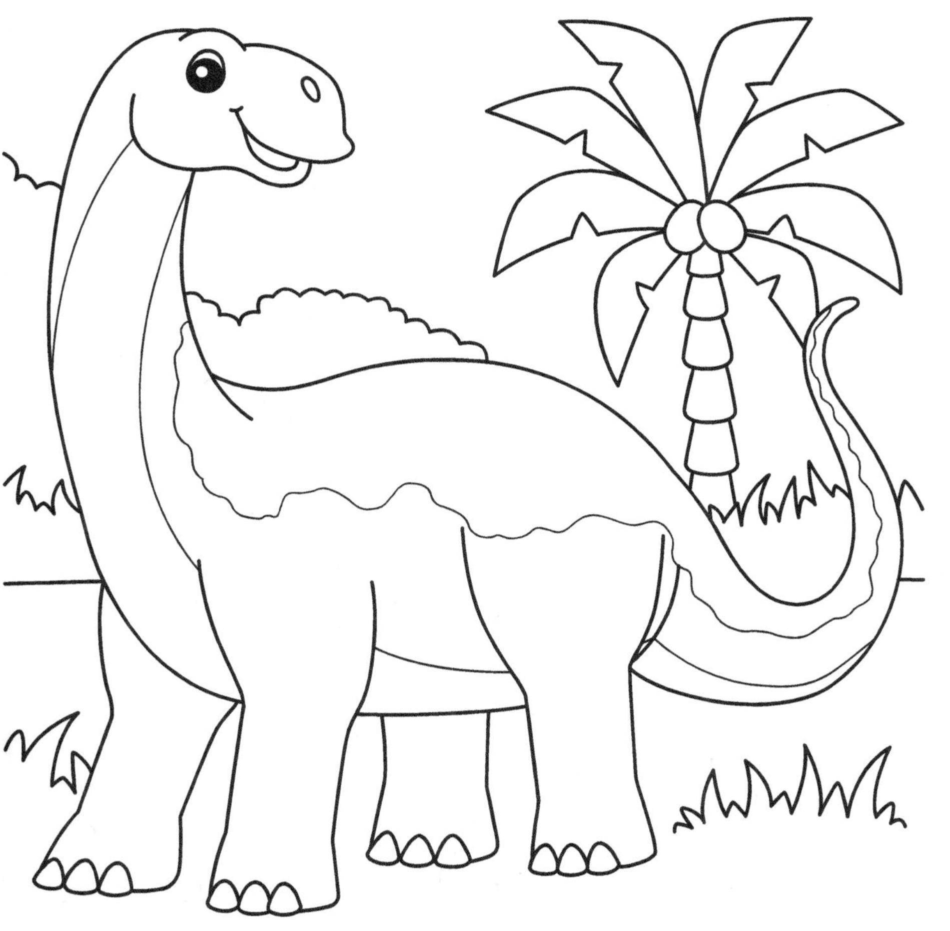

A jobaria was a herbivore
that laid eggs.

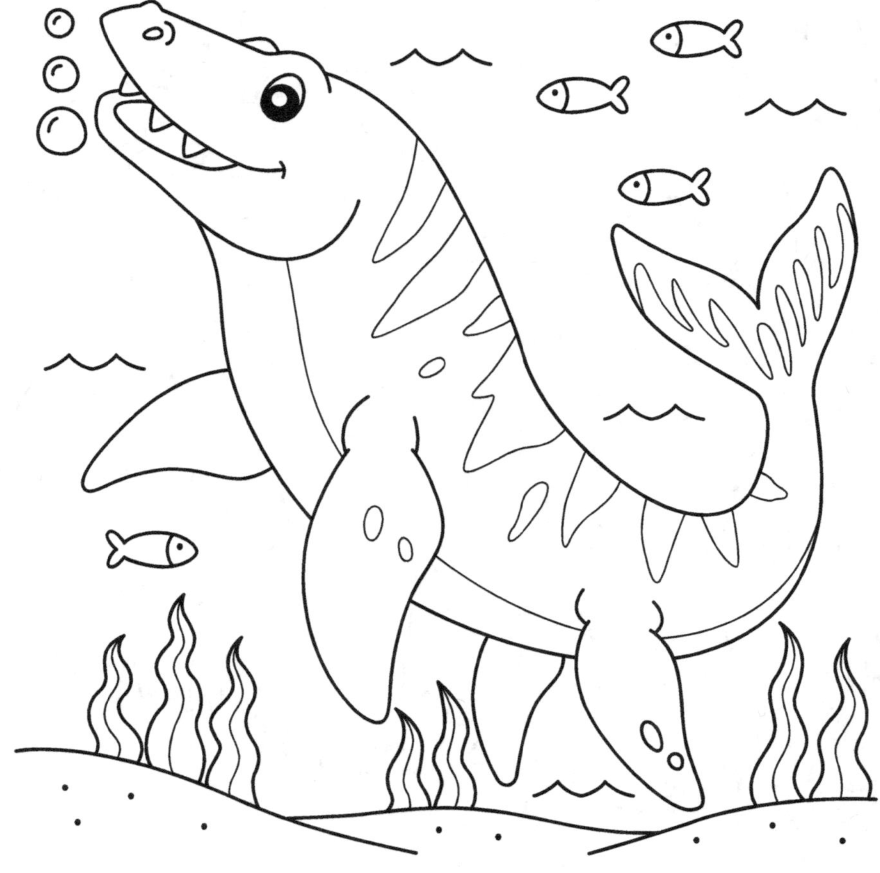

A mosasaurus was found in oceans worldwide.

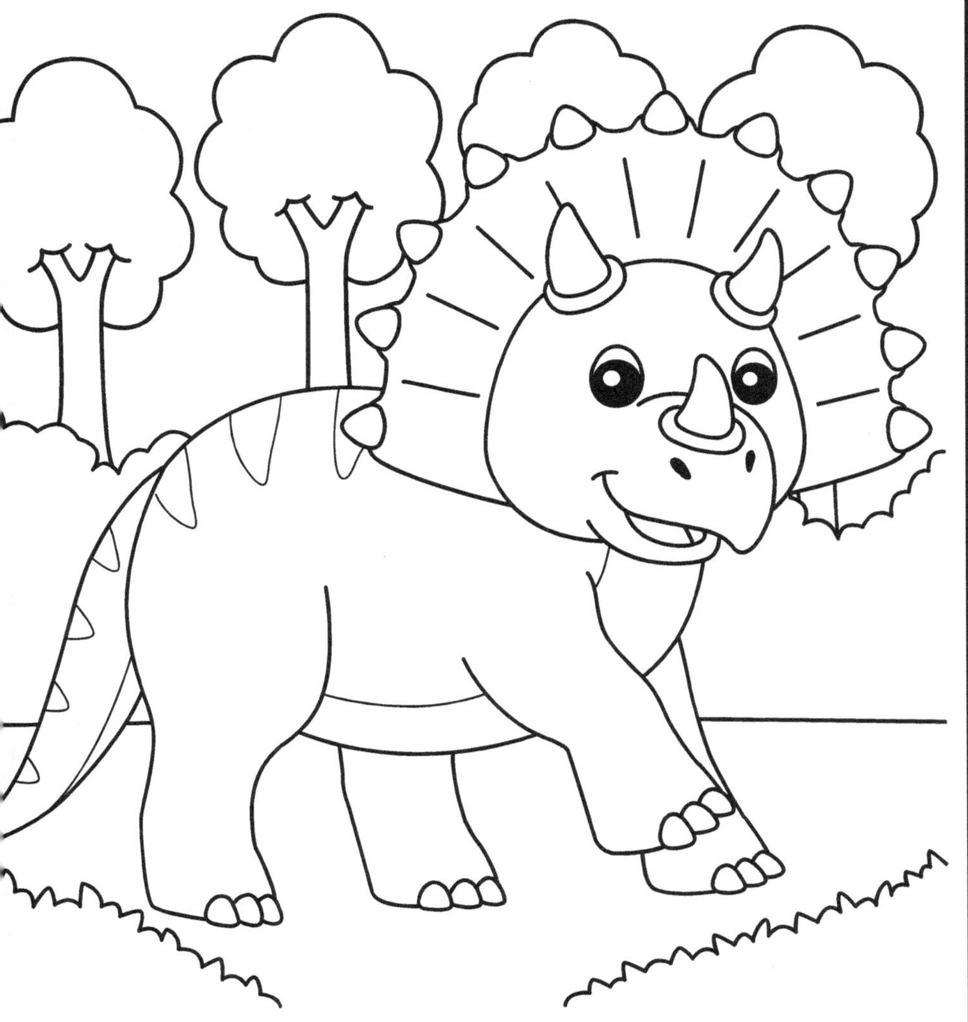

A triceratops's mouth
acted like scissors.

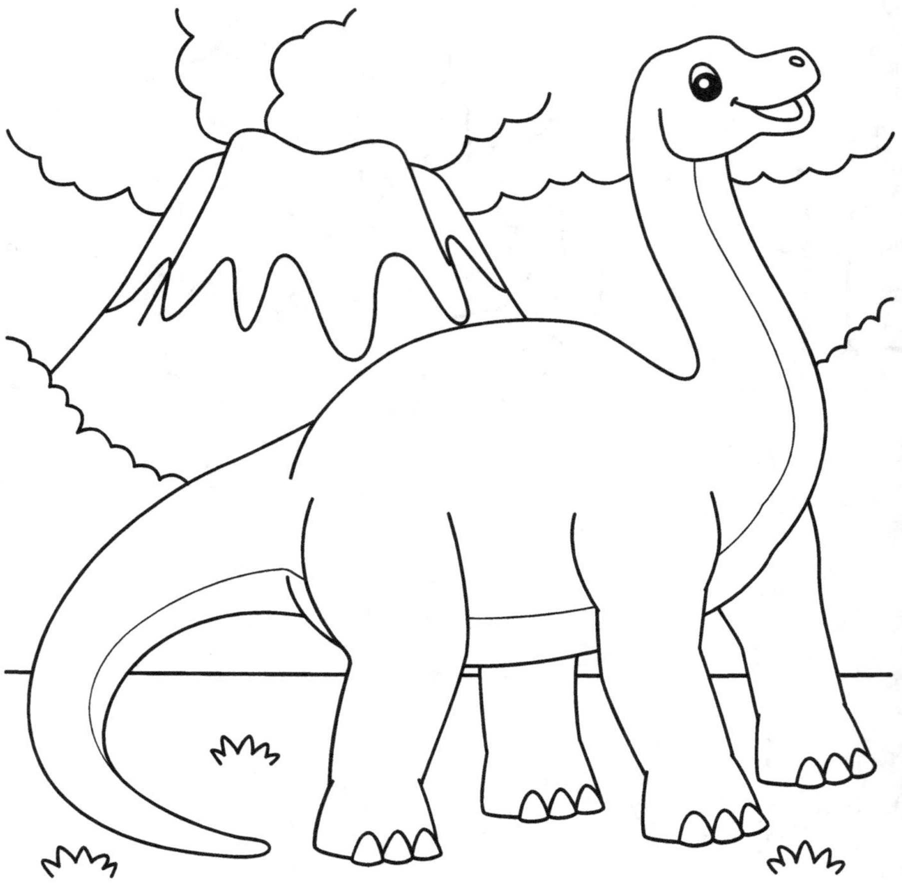

A brontosaurus weighed
about 33 tonnes.

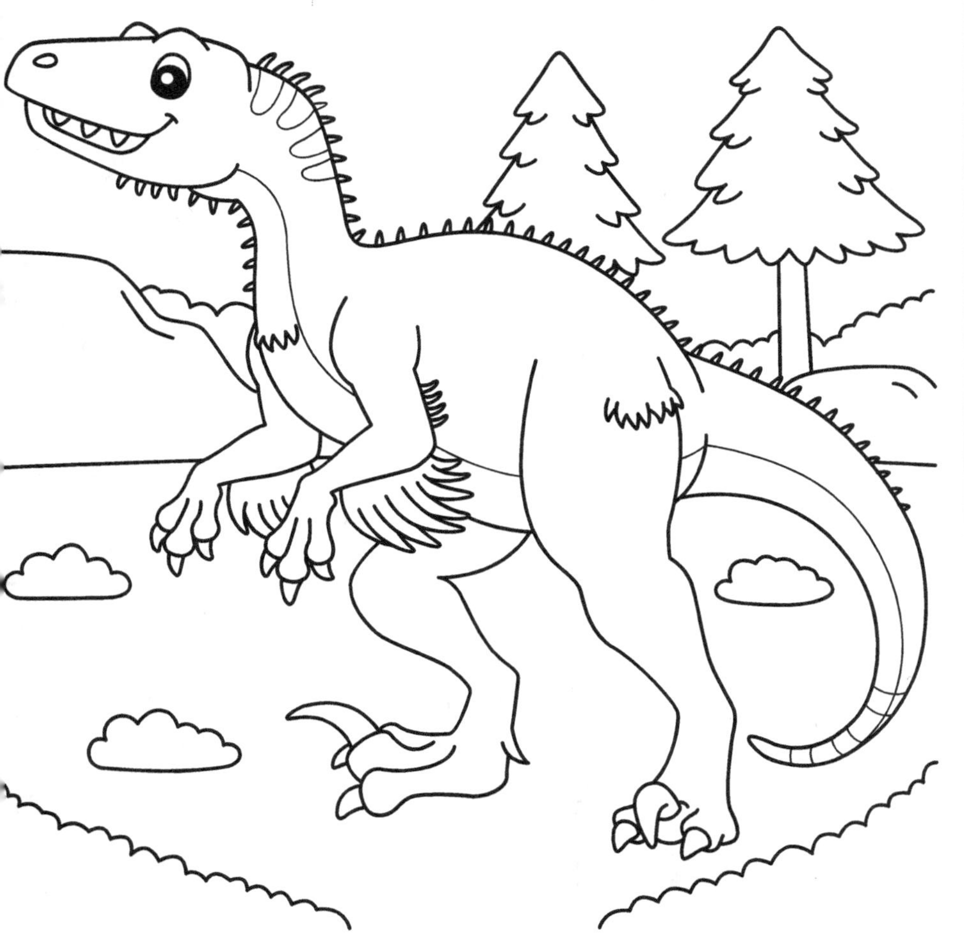

A utahraptor could jump 15 feet high.

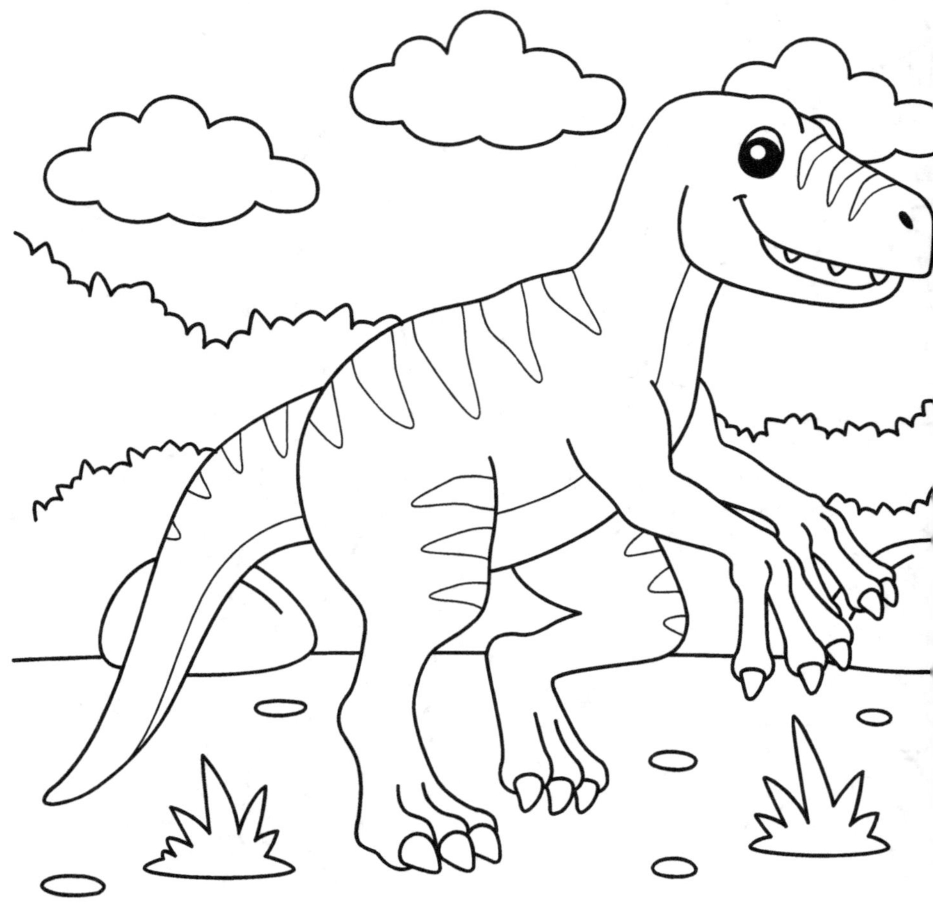

A velociraptor could run
increibly fast.

lufengosaurus

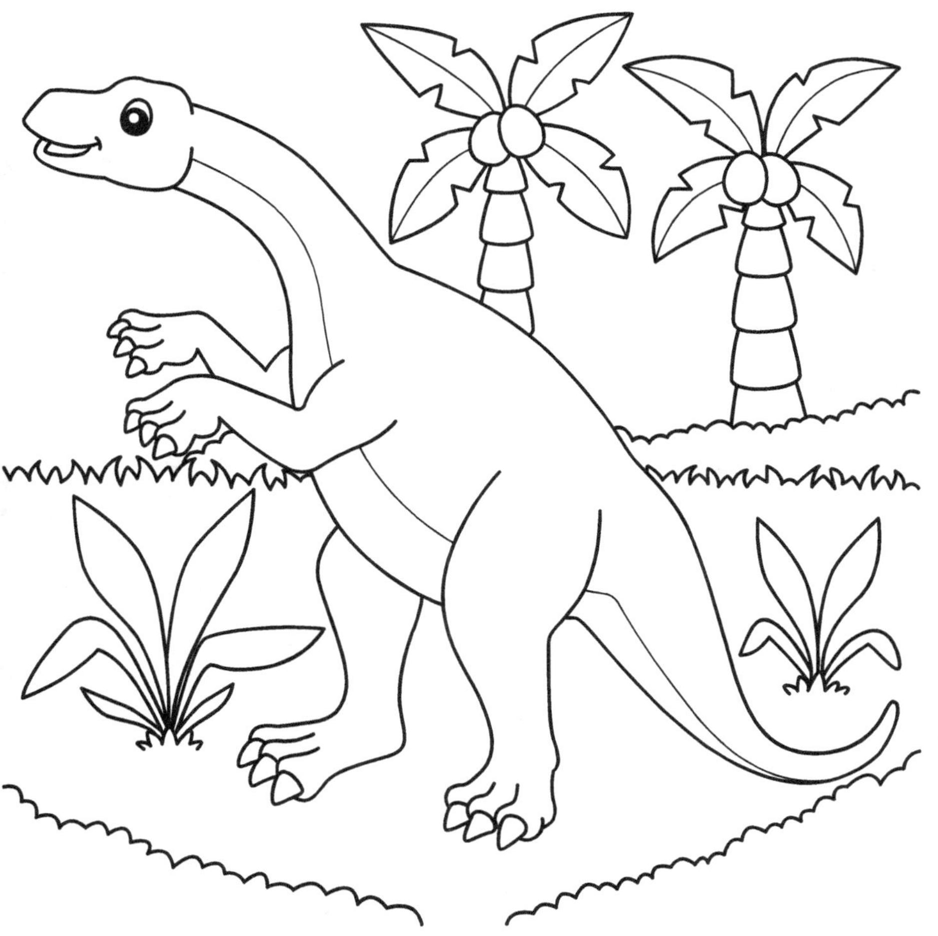

A lufengosaurus was a
herbivore.

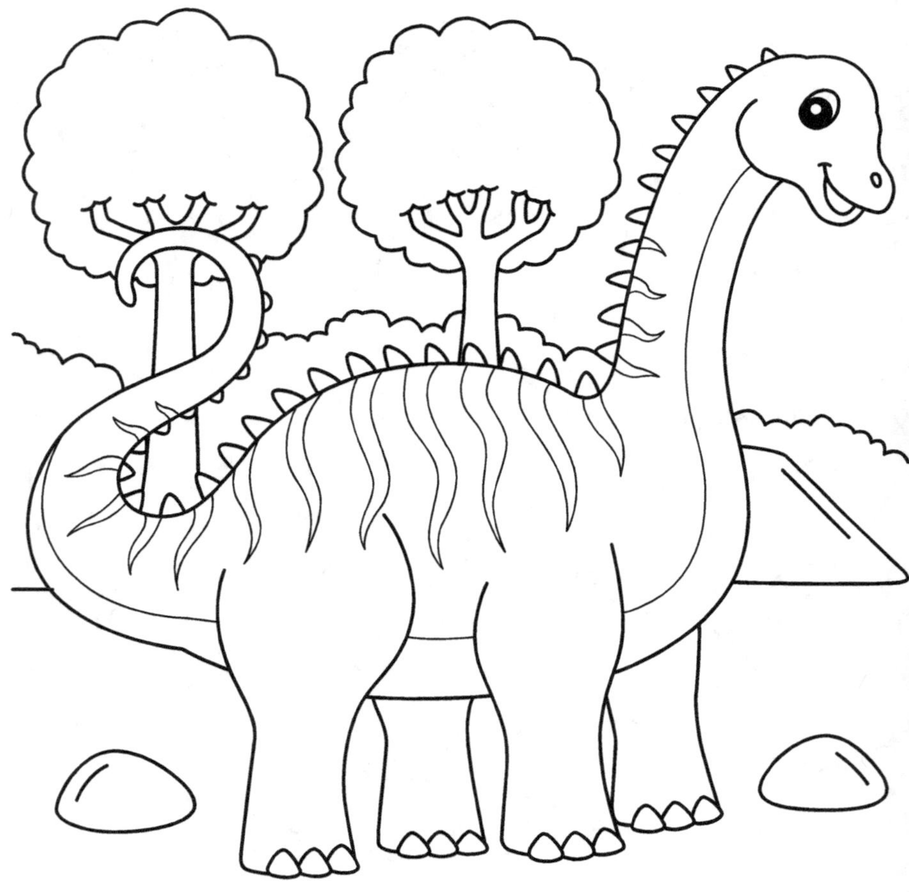

Diplodocus means 'double beamed lizard'.

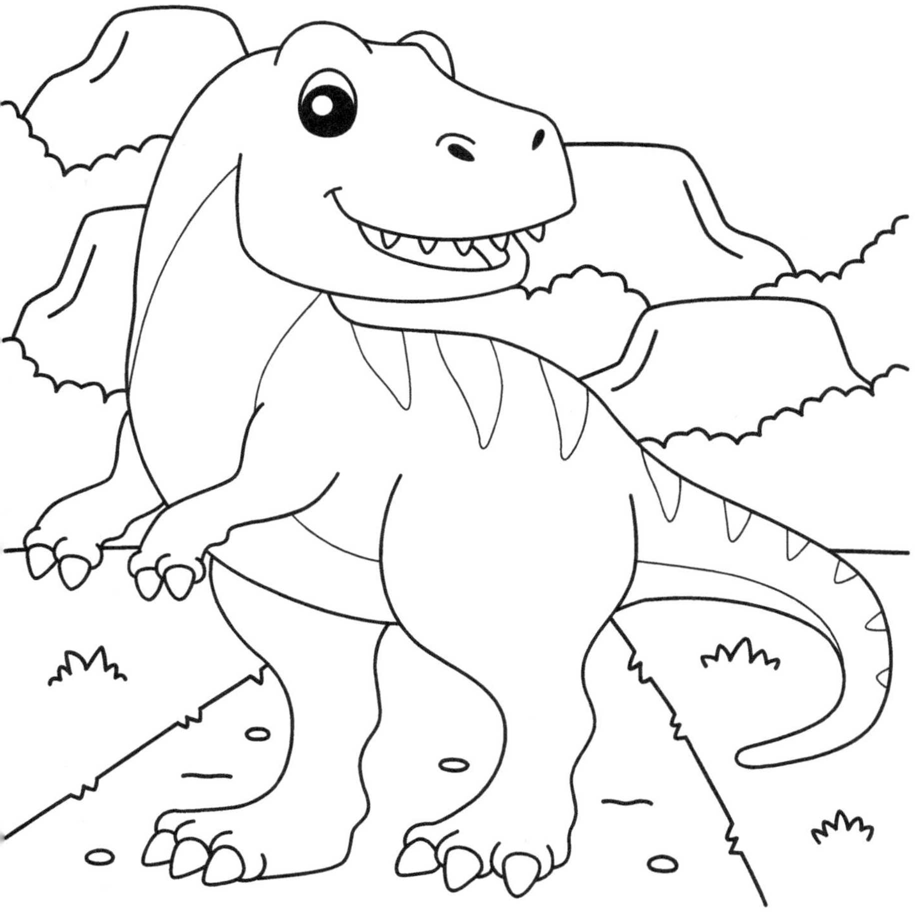

Tyrannosaurus means
'tyrant lizard'.

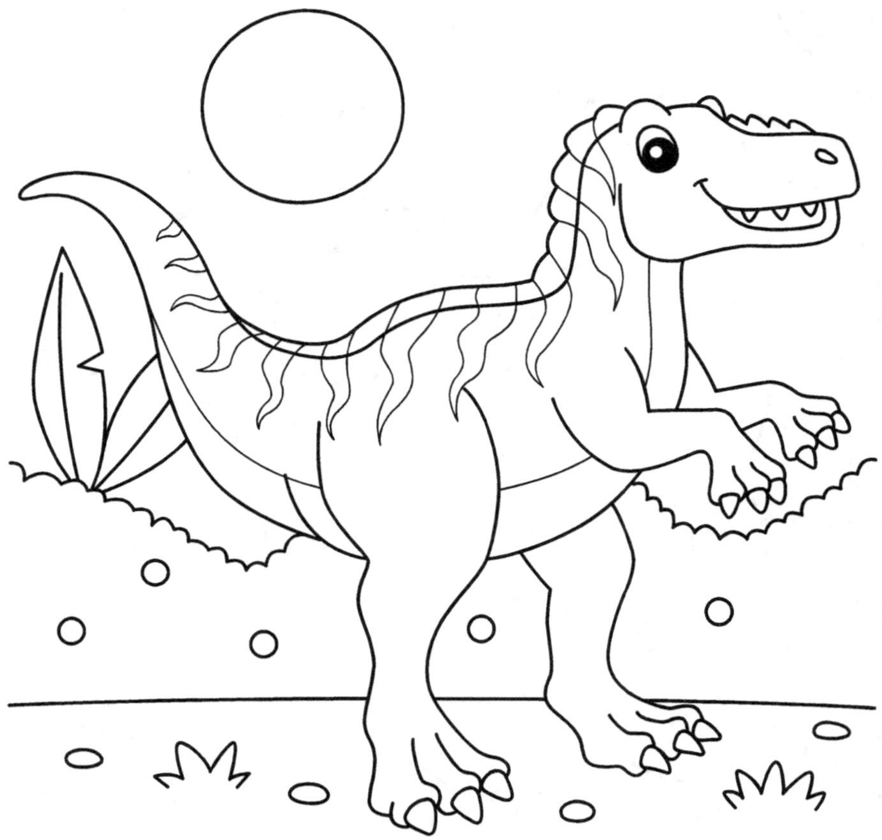

A fukuiraptor lived about
136 million years ago.

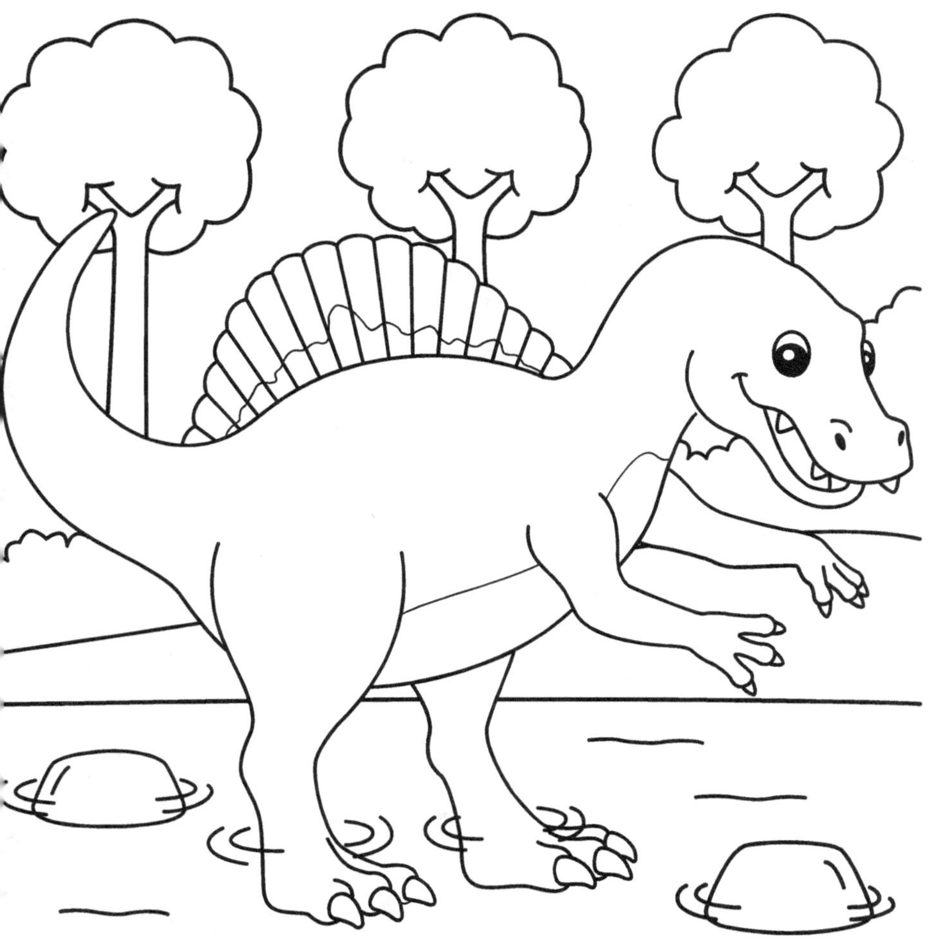

A spinosaurus was the largest land predator.

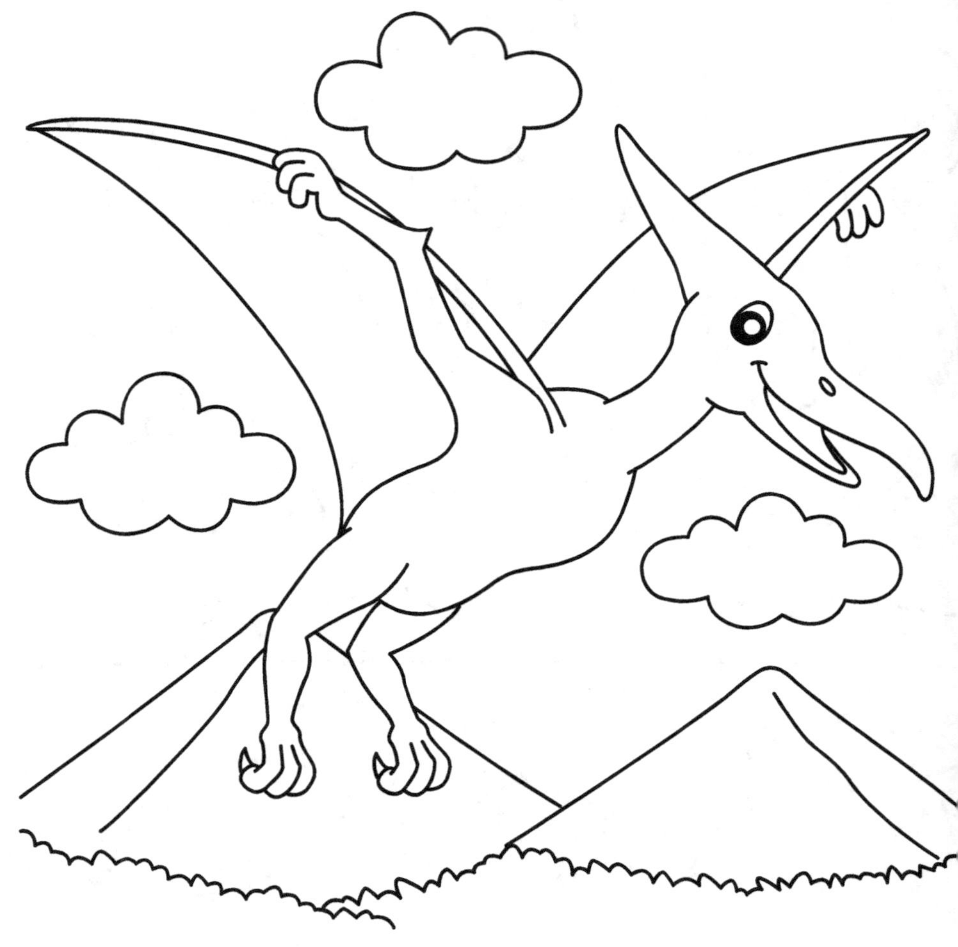

A pterodactyl was a flying reptile.

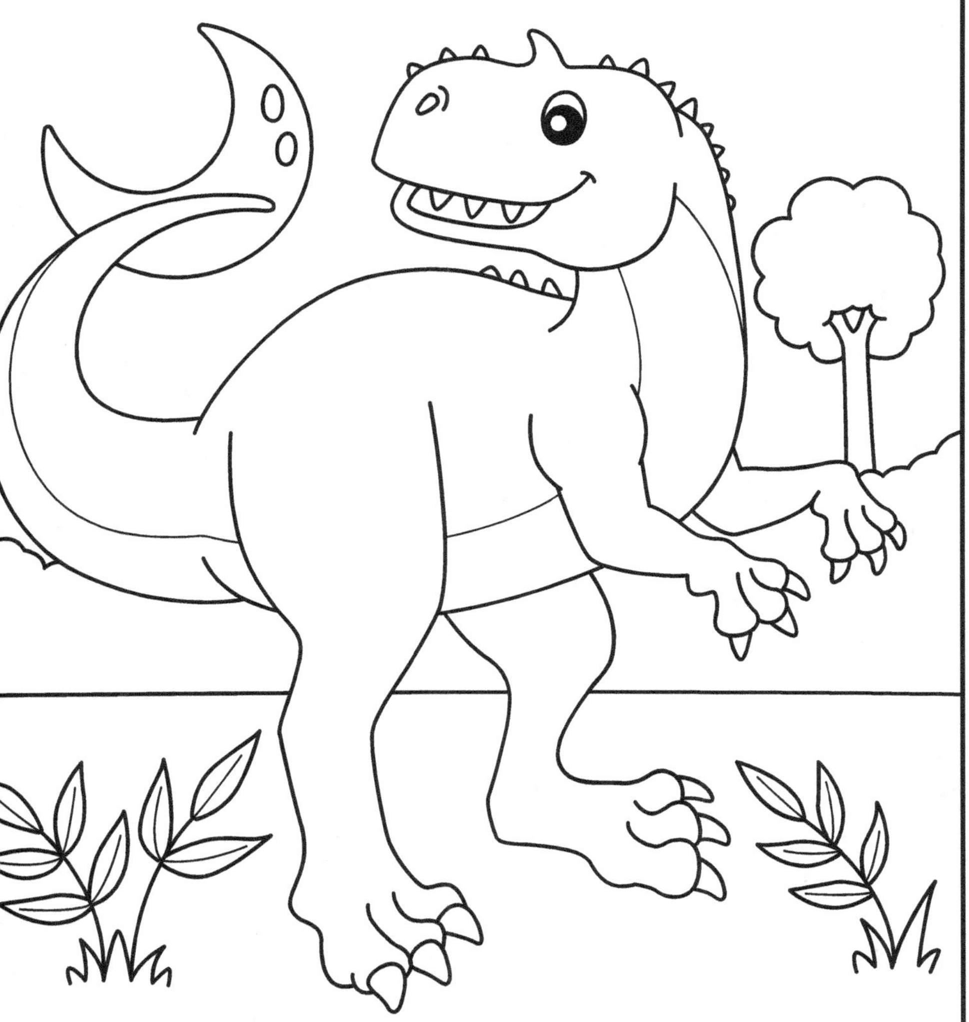# rajasaurus

A rajasaurus was a
carnivore that laid eggs.

kentrosaurus

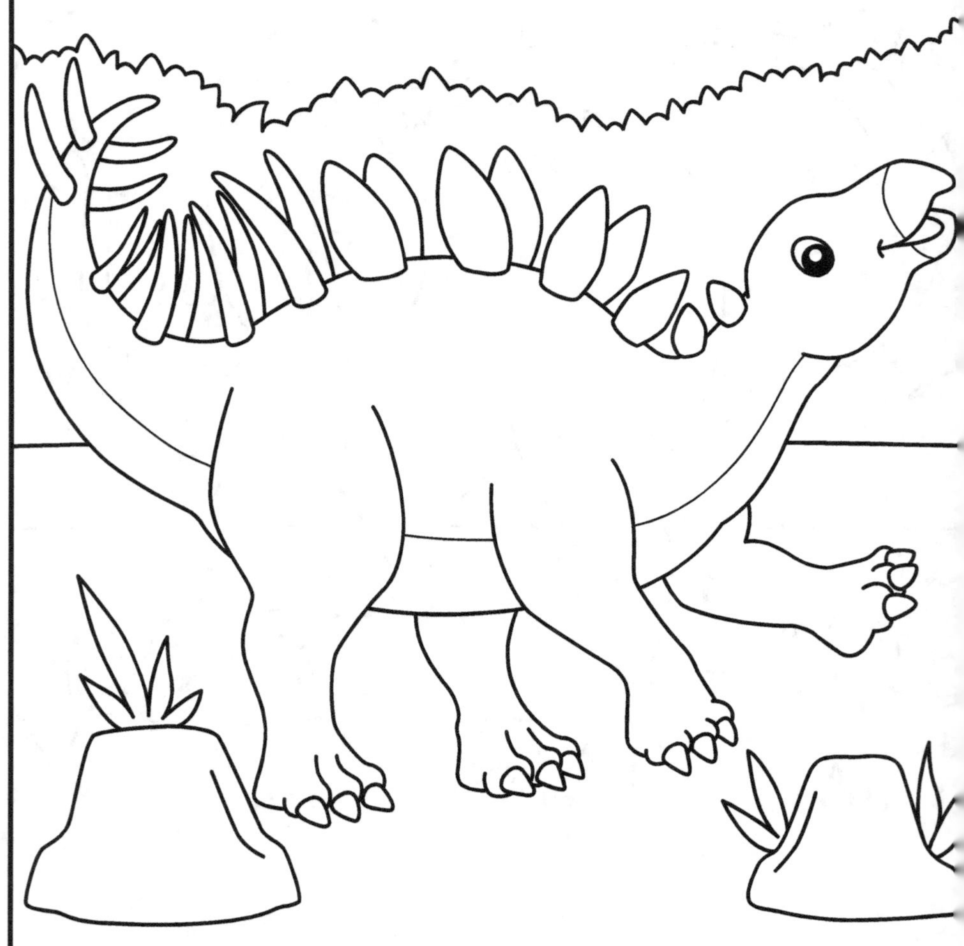

Kentrosaurus means 'spiked lizard'.

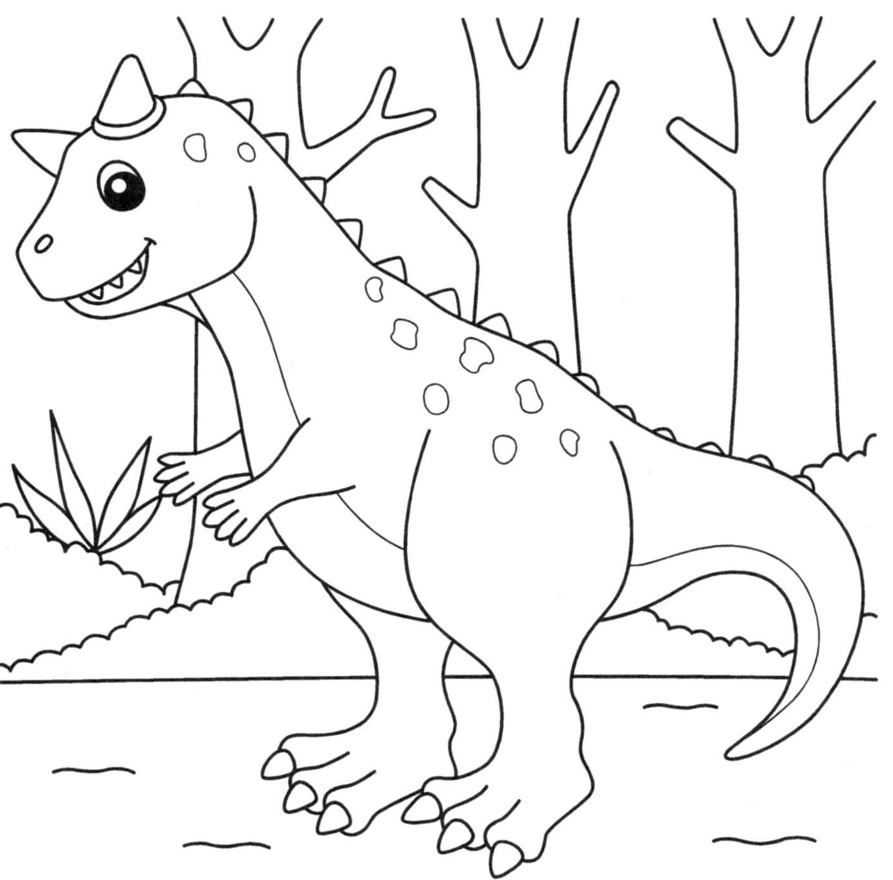

A carnotsaurus had tiny
arms and could run fast.

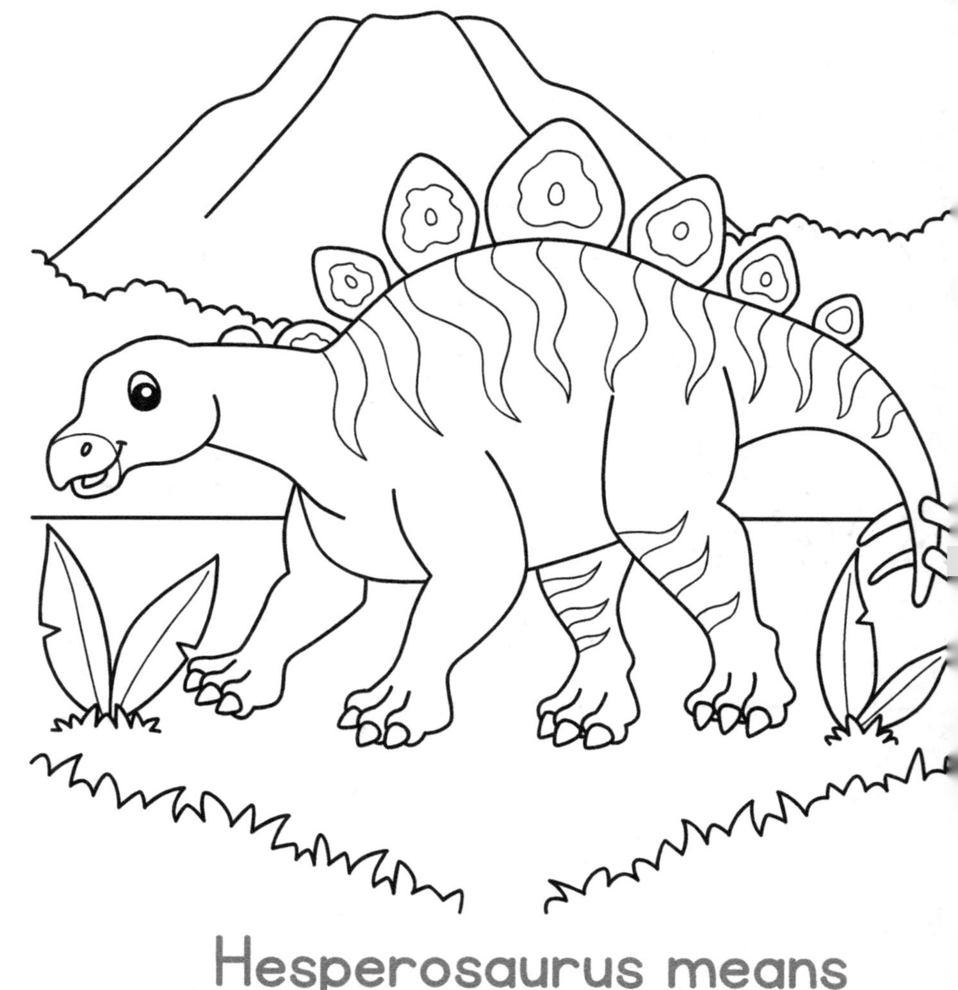

Hesperosaurus means
'western lizard'.

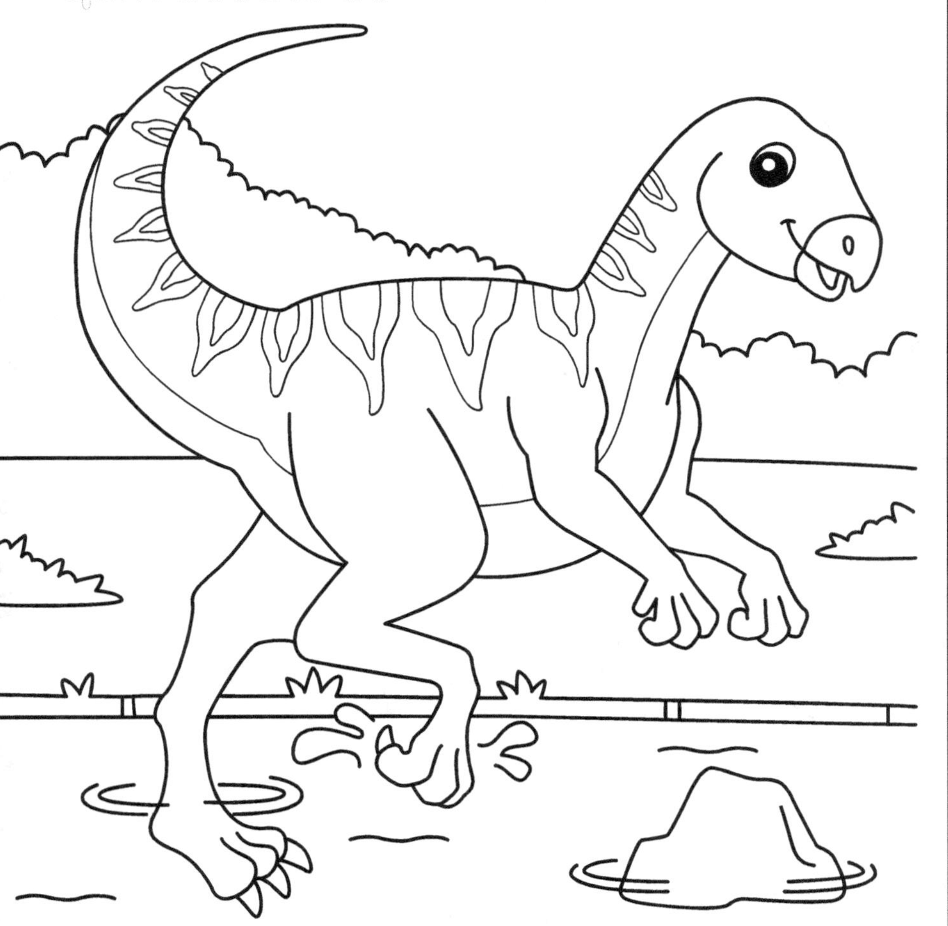

A qantassaurus lived in Australia.

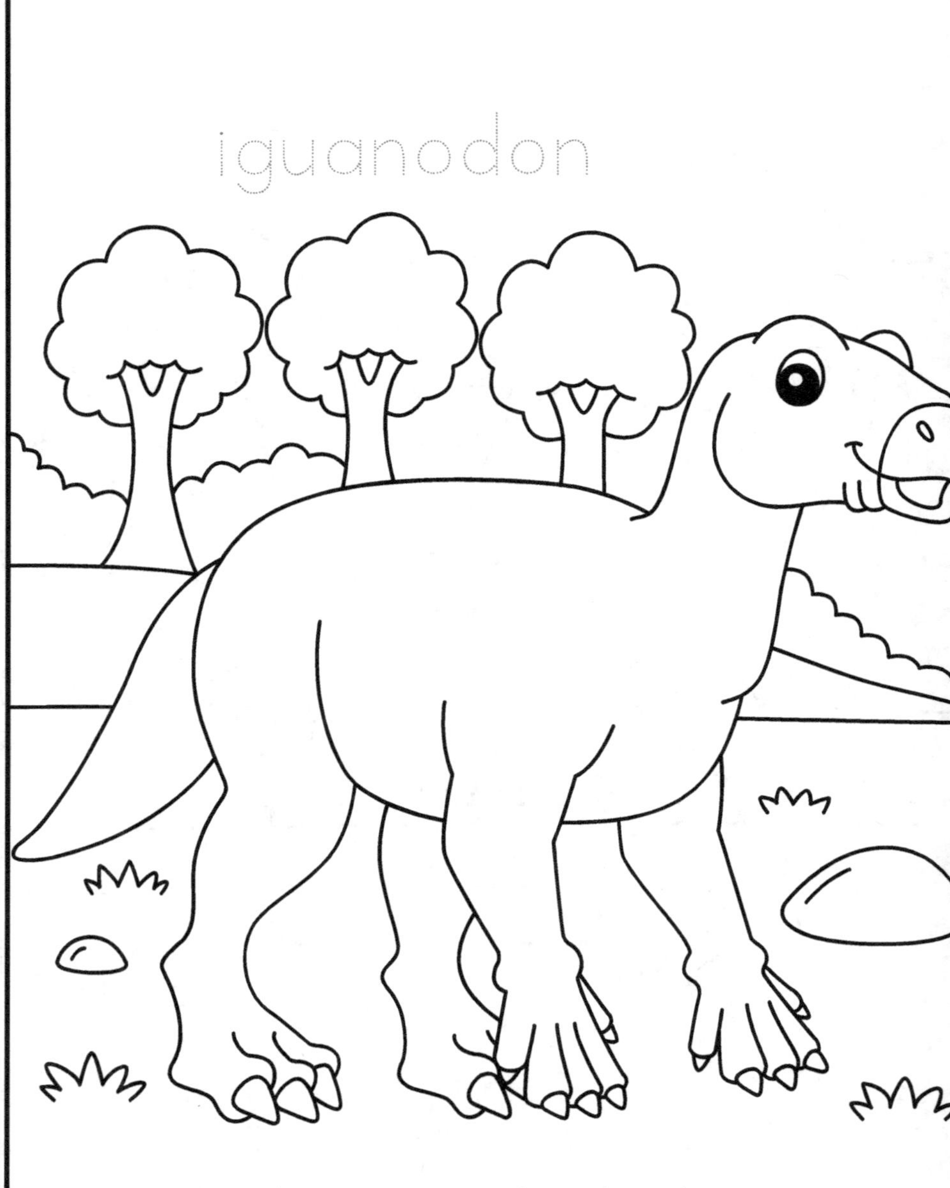

An iguanodon had a
toothless beak.

neuquensaurus

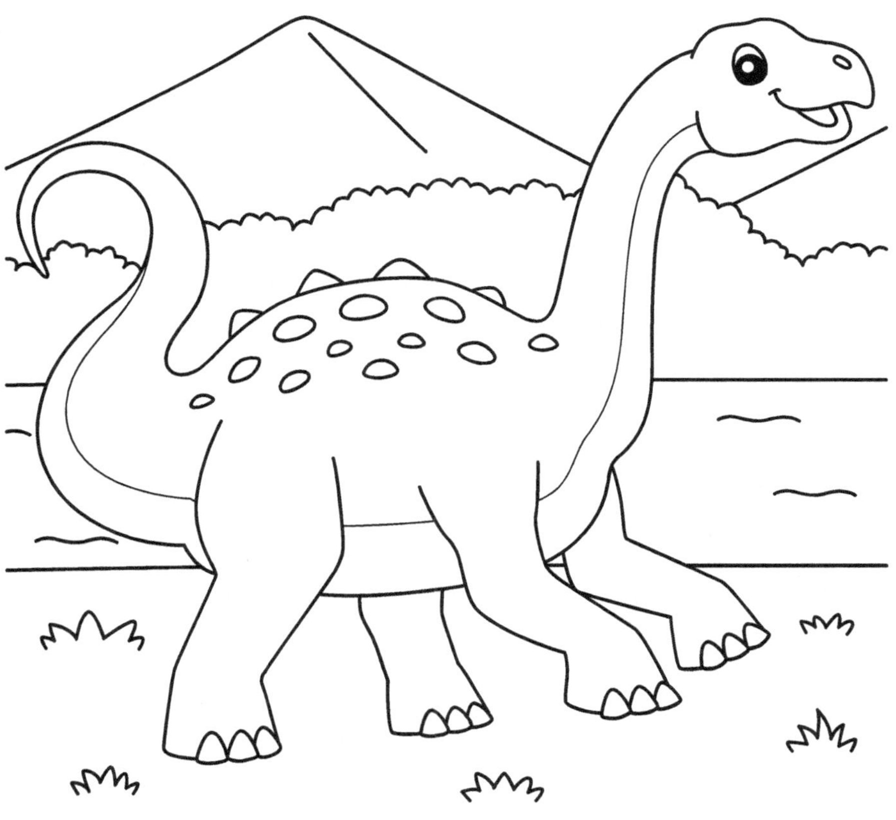

A neuquensaurus moved
using all four legs.

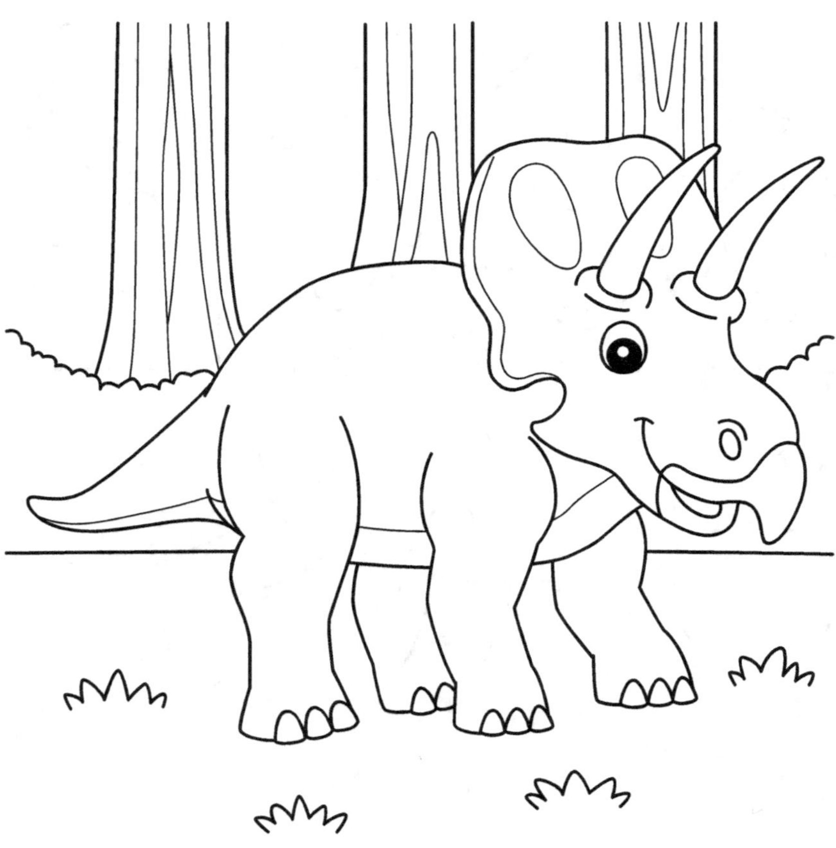

A zuniceratops was a small herbivore.

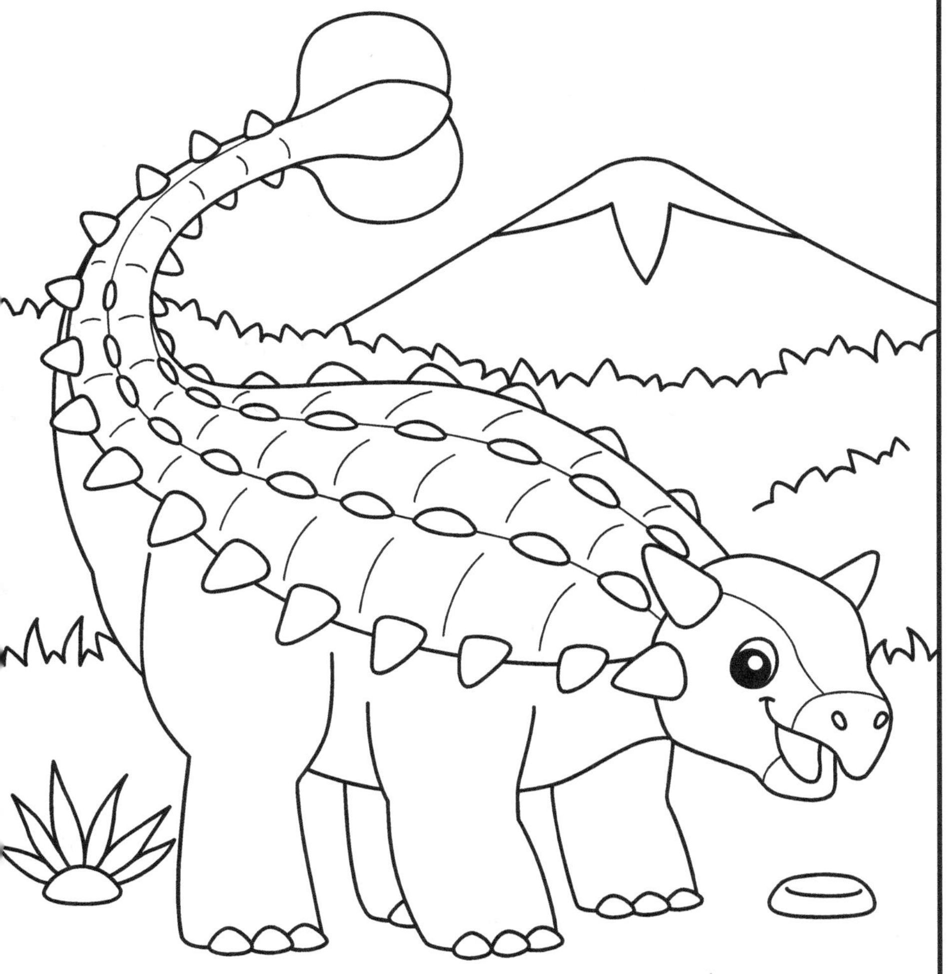

An ankylosaurus had a very small brain.

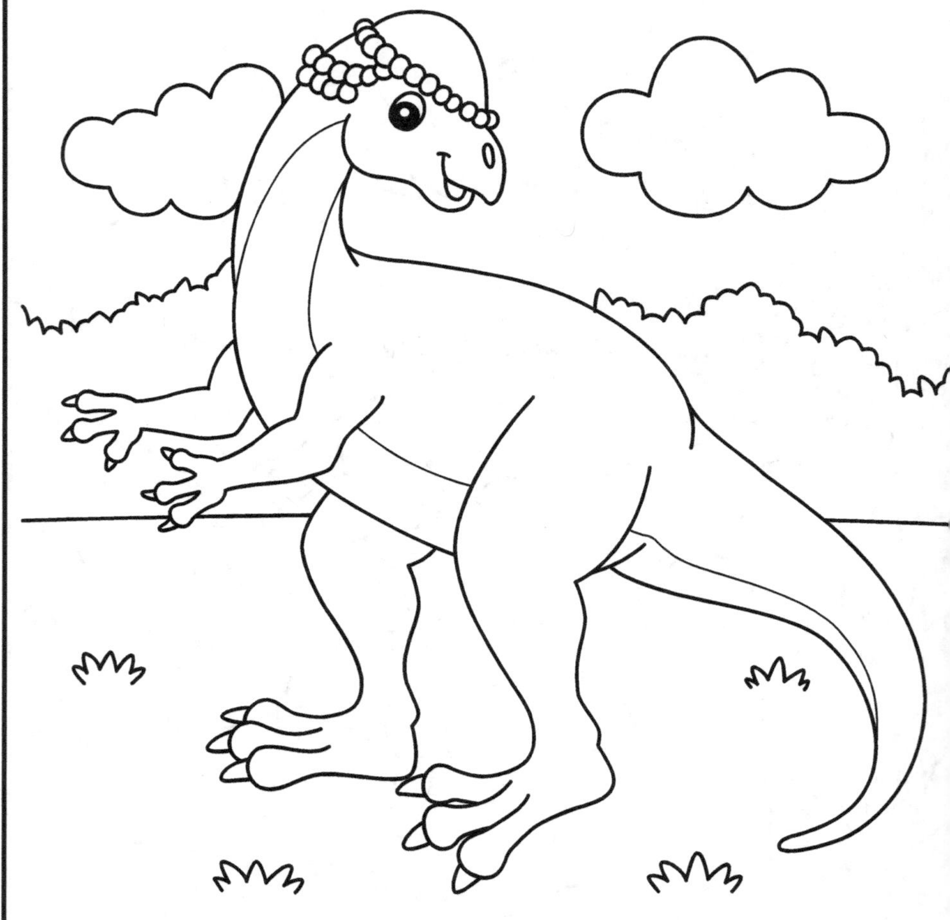

A wannanosaurus lived
about 70 million years ago.

Thank you

It was nice having you on this adventure.